1977

EEN DAYS

h day the book is kept overtime.

BEYOND THE BALANCE SHEET

evaluating profit potential

BEYOND THE
BALANCE SHEET

evaluating profit potential

James Lines
Managing Director, Rank Radio International Limited

BUSINESS BOOKS LIMITED
London

First published 1974

©JAMES LINES 1974

ISBN 0 220 66249 5

LC# 74-5512

This book has been set in 11 on 13 Times Roman
by Redwood Burn Limited
for the publishers, Business Books Limited
(registered office: 110 Fleet Street, London EC4)
publishing offices: Mercury House, Waterloo Road, London SE1

Photoset, printed and bound
in Great Britain by
REDWOOD BURN LIMITED
Trowbridge & Esher

CONTENTS

ACKNOWLEDGEMENTS

Many of the ideas presented in this book were developed jointly with colleagues in TEAM (Investment Appraisals) Limited. As in most situations in which a group of people work together in a common field, it is difficult to know, later on, how each of the individual ideas originated, so I express my general appreciation of their contribution rather than attempt to identify individuals.

The work done by Stanley Linden in constructively criticizing the first draft of this book and making me rewrite the obscure passages has been as valuable to me as it must have been tedious for him, and I thank him for it. The work of Alan Bartlett in the field of Corporate Philosophy has also been helpful in sharpening the idea of 'the underlying strengths of a business' to the more precise and useful concept of 'distinctive competence'.

No doubt I have also built on the work of many other management writers, and I have included reference to some relevant and helpful books in the bibliography.

PREFACE

During my career as a management consultant I have often encountered situations in which a recently acquired business or a new investment has turned out to be a good deal less attractive than was expected, even to the extent of becoming a serious problem. Usually it has proved possible to remedy the situation with considerable management effort, but sometimes the results have hardly seemed to justify the original investment.

Many of these situations had arisen because the decision to invest had been taken almost entirely on the basis of past profit performance, or to obtain tangible assets at a discount, but with only a superficial look beyond the balance sheet at the underlying circumstances of the business.

Many of the problems would have been avoided had there been a detailed study of the business in order to obtain a thorough understanding of its strengths and weaknesses and to form a rounded judgement about its profit potential.

This book, which is based on experience of carrying out such studies in a wide range of industries, describes how they can be carried out and discusses some of the problems that may arise along the way. It is intended to help managers who have a need to make such appraisals in the normal course of managing their businesses, or when aquisitions or investments in new projects are being considered.

Chapter One

INTRODUCTION

The fundamental preoccupation of all businessmen is a search for ways of improving the profitability of their businesses. The level of profitability achieved is regarded by the business community as a primary indicator of performance and in extreme cases profit improvement may be essential for survival. A well run business has, of course, many other objectives besides the raw pursuit of profit: it is satisfying the needs of customers, suppliers, employees and the community at large, as well as those of its shareholders. But, as its ability to earn profits affects its performance in all other fields, profitability must be a central pre-occupation of management.

The search for profit growth normally has two aspects:

1 The improvement of performance in existing fields of business.
2 Investment in new projects of high profit potential.

In the long term it is the latter of these two activities that determines a company's rate of profit growth. It has been said by Peter Drucker among others, that business success comes from identifying and exploiting opportunities, rather than from solving problems. Profit growth depends therefore primarily on allocating resources preferentially to projects of high profit potential. The other necessary skill, that of releasing the profit potential that has been identified, can be brought into play only at a secondary stage. The successful evaluation of profit potential is therefore an important determinant of business success.

Within a single company there may be several divisions, or separate product groups, each demanding resources —management attention; design, marketing and manu- facturing skills; production capacity; finance to fund the necessary inventories; etc. Often there is not enough money available to finance each of the opportunities and the question arises: should funds be provided to any of them, if so which one?

Even if the problem is not one of discriminating between investment possibilities, it is necessary to decide whether a pro- ject is satisfactory in its own right in order to justify the use of the necessary resources.

Companies that are growing by acquisition will constantly need to examine possible new investments to ensure that their choice of partners is valid and that their profit performance is therefore enhanced by each merger rather than the reverse.

In a loss-making company it can be important to decide whether the company can recover from the situation, or should be put into liquidation while there are still some funds available for creditors and shareholders.

In each of these situations the fundamental need is the same —to estimate, with reasonable precision, the profitability that can be expected from the business under review, during a suc- cession of future dates. Other circumstances are, of course, not uniform, nor is the amount of information available to the person carrying out the assessment. An orderly system for the assessment of profit potential must therefore be a flexible one so that it can be used in a wide range of circumstances.

Reduction of uncertainty

Any business is a complex entity and the factors that lead to success are not all measurable. It consists of:

    1 Plant, buildings, stocks and other physical assets which

can be measured and counted and valued.
2 People and their relationships which can be studied but not measured with any worthwhile precision.
3 Completely intangible concepts, like reputation, market image, management culture, which can be assessed but certainly not quantified.

The only things that are known with reasonable precision about a business are its present tangible worth and its past profit performance. All other knowledge is necessarily imprecise and not primarily capable of assessment in financial terms. Yet it is these intangibles that really determine whether a company will grow and increase its rate of profit, or decline and possibly become insolvent. The evaluation of profit potential is therefore concerned as much with getting the best possible understanding of the intangible factors as it is with empirical measurement.

It follows that a systematic assessment can materially reduce the uncertainty surrounding forecasts of future profitability in a way that would not be possible by a purely arithmetical projection. It cannot, of course, entirely eliminate such uncertainty.

Internal investment

In order to decide between alternative uses of funds within a group or company, it is necessary to form a judgement about the potential profitability of the projects under review. Usually such projects are concerned with designing, manufacturing and marketing a group of products, or developing and marketing a new service. In such a situation all management activities are involved and therefore a rounded assessment is necessary.

In the case of individual, small projects, such as the installation of a single item of plant or manufacturing process, the use of discounted cash flow techniques provides the mechanism for calculating the theoretical benefit in allocating funds to the project. This is, however, only a means of calculation. It is the underlying assumptions that provide the raw data for the calculations, and which really determine the outcome. For example: 'Can the products arising from a new process continue to be sold over the assumed life of the plant required?' The assumption that this is possible is a bold one to make without a very careful examination of the underlying market trends. 'Can the individuals working on the project manage it successfully and deal with the problems that will necessarily arise? Will the cash inflow be controlled by the production learning curve or by the market growth curve?'

Even in such a simple case as an investment in an individual manufacturing process, the assessment of profit potential is far from an easy one. If, instead of being concerned with a single process, the project is a complete new field of business, then the factors involved are much more varied and the assessment process correspondingly more complex.

Within a company the assessment of profit potential is closely linked with long-term business planning. A corporate plan is normally a statement of the way it is intended to release the profit potential inherent in the business. In the establishment of such a plan any weakness in carrying out an assessment of profit potential can lead to areas of attractive potential being disregarded in favour of less attractive alternatives.

The assessment of profit potential of various parts of a company's business is, therefore, a fundamental part of its corporate planning process and is particularly important in companies that are engaged in more than one field of business.

External investment

Within a business, there is ample opportunity to monitor performance against the forecast and, if there is departure from the forecast level of profitability, action can be initiated to remedy the situation. An external investor is not in this comfortable position of being able to take direct action to safeguard his funds, should the investment not appear to be as profitable as was hoped. It is therefore even more important for such an investor to carry out a thorough appraisal of profit potential before placing his money at risk.

It is not possible to do this in depth if the investment is by means of acquiring Ordinary shares on the Stock Exchange, but if the investment is in a private company or is in the form of an injection of loan capital into a public company, then a detailed appraisal is always a wise precaution.

There are, of course, special circumstances which can result in a short-term benefit from an investment which is largely fortuitous. For example, a company may have properties that are worth more than their book value, or stocks and basic materials that have risen in value because of changes in world prices; but these are exceptions to the general rule. In most normal situations an investor who wishes to obtain a high rate of return on his investment, coupled with security, can obtain those benefits in the long run only by investing in companies that are able to achieve a sustained rate of profit growth.

Acquisitions and mergers

If there is an opportunity to acquire by negotiation another business, then obviously a very careful exploration is required. The acquirer needs a knowledge of all the attributes of the business which have made it successful in the past: management strengths, market position, products, skills, reputation, forward plan. . . . A rounded picture of the company can be built up partly by collecting factual data, partly by objective observation and partly by informed judgement. The company initiating the merger can then consider how far the proposed acquisition would meet its defined needs and make the decision on a sound basis.

One important aspect of such a situation is that the investor will presumably have control of the situation after making the acquisition. He will need to assess, therefore, not just the profit potential of the business in its existing management situation, but what its potential would be as part of his own business, and also how far that business would change as a result of the merger. The strengths of both parties to the merger are therefore important. There will, however, be an opportunity to monitor progress and change the business plans from time to time.

If it is less than full control that is under consideration, then there will be little or no opportunity to change plans later. In this case, an assessment of the profit potential of the business in its present form is even more important and the penalty for error is more severe.

In either of the above situations the amount of information revealed to a potential investor can vary considerably. If the acquiring company is in the same business there may be a reluctance to reveal too much before the agreement is finalized. In this case, perceptive judgements have to be made from limited information.

In most cases it must be assumed that there will be a tendency for the management of the business under study to present a more favourable picture than the circumstances really warrant. The degree to which this occurs can vary from fraudulent at one extreme, to the use of minor euphemisms at the other. It can be assumed, however, that adverse information will not be presented unless the appropriate questions are asked. It is up to the potential investor to make sure that the questions are asked.

In the case of a bid by one public company for another, information may be much more limited. There may be no opportunity to obtain information from within the company. Usually, all the bidder knows is what has been published in the Press, and is common knowledge in the financial community and within the industry in question. He must rely on what he can find out by a study of generally available information.

Without behaving unethically or engaging in industrial espionage, there is still a great deal that can be done to find out the company's strengths as a basis for an assessment of profit potential. For example, the product range is known and it is not difficult to find out about the rate of product innovation: the market can be researched and the company's market share established and customer attitudes can be explored. A detailed examination of individual products will provide a great deal of information about the company's manufacturing competence and the level of design skills. It should, in skilled hands, even permit cost calculations to be made.

Therefore, although it is not possible to carry out a full evaluation in an opposed bid situation, it is certainly possible to find out a great deal more than is normally attempted and, therefore, to be much more precise in the evaluation of potential, and in the identification of likely development requirements.

Disposal of a business

Considerations of profit potential are also paramount in deciding whether or not to dispose of an unsuccessful business or even to close it down. In general there is a tendency amongst managers to try to hold on through a period of losses, in the belief that the business will eventually return to profitability. This is a natural attitude; as the livelihood and reputation of the managers is at stake, they will not lightly give up a struggle to regain a satisfactory level of profitability.

If they are wrong about the recovery prospects, or if recovery takes longer than was expected, the business may build up losses that will require many years of profitable trading to offset. It can, therefore, be a mistake to persist too long in trying to resolve the problems of an unprofitable business.

It is not suggested that the moment a business temporarily ceases to be profitable it should be closed down; but certainly its profit potential should be examined in considerable depth to make sure that it is likely to become profitable again. If the answer is unfavourable, then the sooner the decision is made the better will be the chance of containing the losses. If the decision is to sell, it is best to do so before all the company's assets have been drained away.

Objectives

To recapitulate, businesses have as many objectives as there are individuals involved. To a customer a business exists to supply a product or a service; to a supplier it is an outlet for his product; to employees it is a source of income and job satisfaction; to a shareholder it is a source of income and capital growth. All of these, however, are dependent on the business earning profit at sufficient level to provide funds for future development, to build up reserves as a security against future circumstances and to generate a favourable cash flow to offset inflation.

The purpose of this book is to suggest the process by which the profit potential of a business can be explored in a systematic way in order to reduce some of the uncertainty in planning and investment decisions. It has been assumed that the appraiser has access to the business and can freely discuss its future with members of the management team. Where this is only possible to a limited extent, or not possible at all, it becomes much more difficult to form reliable conclusions; but even in this situation some of the questions suggested in the book can be answered by reference to generally available information. The chapters that follow describe how an appraisal can be conducted, warn of some of the problems that may be encountered and suggest a range of exploratory questions that may be asked during an appraisal.

If one accepts that the primary objective of a business is to create wealth (without arguing too much about the semantic use of the word 'create') then the assessment of profit potential must be somewhere near the heart of the development of a successful business strategy.

Chapter Two

EXTRAPOLATION – THE TRADITIONAL APPROACH

There is one conventional approach to the assessment of profit potential that is widely used amongst companies when they are contemplating acquisition or investment in another business. This, in essence, is to examine in considerable detail what the company has achieved in the past, to establish trend lines, and then to project those trends into the future.

Normally an accountant's report is obtained. This usually gives an outline history of the company, particularly in financial terms, but also including some background information on products, management, etc. It highlights the main trends of turnover, profit, etc., over a number of years (the number depending on the company's history, but usually up to ten years is shown). It also provides a great deal of information about the company's current assets, particularly with regard to the way these have been valued.

On the basis of such a report, projections of future performance are made based on extrapolating the existing trends. Usually some validation of the trends is attempted and obvious changes of circumstance are allowed for, but seldom is a real attempt made to look beyond the figures or make any qualitative judgements except of the broadest kind. Many investments are made, and companies bought, on such limited information.

Within companies also, this method is often used by individual managers. It is possibly the rule rather than the exception that budgets are prepared in this way. The company finds its turnover has increased by ten per cent in each of the three or four preceding years and therefore adds another ten per cent for the next year, without really knowing why it has expanded in the previous years or whether the same forces will continue to operate. A company needs growth to satisfy its shareholders, and so it budgets for growth without doing the detailed studies to demonstrate how it can be done or whether it can be done.

Some use of past trends as a means of predicting the future is a very well established practice. It rests on the assumption that a company acquires a certain momentum, so that if it has been successful in the past it will continue to be successful in the future. There is some validity in this assumption, particularly for short-term forecasts. If a company is well managed and there is continuity of management, there is a good reason to assume it will go on being successful; if it sells high quality products which satisfy customer needs, then it is fair to assume that those products will go on being sold and probably at much the same level of profitability. However, having accepted that trends can be projected and used as a method of forecasting in some circumstances, it can also be said that this method has often proved to be unreliable in practice. Sudden reversals of fortune are far too frequent for past trends to be regarded in themselves as a reliable guide to future potential.

The management team may change; even if only one or two managers have to be replaced, nobody can forecast without close scrutiny the effect that the change may have on the balance of the management team, on their leadership, on their co-operation and, therefore, on their performance. Existing managers may become ill and their performance decline. The outside environment may change and a market approach that was once highly effective may suddenly become irrelevant to the changed need. A successful management team with a particular style of management may be the last to recognize the obsolescence of that style. A company whose past success resulted from low-cost manufacturing and low prices for its products, may fail to respond to a market that has become more discriminating about quality.

Market changes

Established products decline; where this happens slowly, one product at a time so that it can be seen to happen, new products can be developed in time to fill the gap. Occasionally, however, a fundamental change is needed to satisfy the market, and any company that does not either anticipate the change or react to it very quickly, will be in trouble, however successful it has been in the past. Examples of such changes are:

1 Replacement of range-finder cameras by single-lens reflex cameras.
2 Replacement of strut jib cranes by telescopic cantilever jib cranes.
3 Replacement of wooden boats by glass-fibre boats.

None of the above changes was an absolute one and none of them happened overnight, but each of them happened rapidly enough to have an appreciable effect on the relative success of companies in the industry and their suppliers, and caused some of them to go into liquidation or unplanned mergers.

Management change

A company owes its success in the long term to a comparatively small group of managers who identify opportunities for growth and then devise a suitable business strategy to take maximum advantage from such opportunities.

Another crucial quality is the ability to turn new ideas into positive achievement. Theodore Levitt makes the point in *The Marketing Mode* that it is relatively easy to produce ideas, but what really counts is getting them carried out in practice, which is a much rarer quality. A really creative man succeeds because of his ability to discriminate between a great number of different ideas, to select only those relevant to his main purpose, and then to get them accepted and implemented despite the opposition and problems that will arise. The difficult part of the process is not thinking of the ideas, it is overcoming the obstacles to their implementation.

The majority of managers in any business are not thinking about business strategy or creatively implementing new ideas. They are concentrating on the day-to-day management of the business, overcoming immediate problems, making detailed improvements in performance and carrying out the very many essential administrative tasks. They must be competent and do their jobs well and they are, of course, essential, but they are much more easily replaceable than the key strategic and creative executives referred to above.

In any business, therefore, there may be a very small number of men who are capable of the key management processes of identifying opportunities for growth, developing an action plan to exploit those opportunities, and of achieving orderly change within the business. In a small company there may be only one man with such qualities.

If such key executives leave, there may be no immediate change in the company's performance. Every company does have a certain business momentum, the routines of management will continue to be carried out by conscientious and hard-working executives, new products will be developed and new markets explored. Outwardly the company will be much as before, but without the key executives its performance will, after a time lag, start to decline, perhaps even to the stage where it is no longer profitable.

In appraising profit potential it is therefore essential to know who are the key executives and whether potential successors are available.

Management complacency

The managers of a business which is highly profitable are apt to become complacent. If, as sometimes happens, their success has been a result of a fortuitous set of circumstances, rather than outstanding management skill, things may go very wrong when the circumstances change. The past success may then, in itself, be harmful by reinforcing resistance to any change in the company's way of doing business.

One example of circumstances that had a fortuitous effect on the results of a number of companies, has been in the recent spate of legislation in most industrialized countries to reduce pollution. The requirement to burn only smokeless fuels in urban areas, gave rise to a very substantial increase in demand which overloaded the existing manufacturing facilities for such fuels, and provided some of the companies concerned with several years of high profitability. In Britain, this was accompanied by the replacement of coal gas by natural gas for domestic and industrial purposes which reduced the supply of smokeless fuel and other by-products of the carbonization of coal.

It may be that the management teams of the companies concerned should be given credit for forecasting the likelihood of clean air legislation, but they could hardly be given credit for forecasting the discovery of North Sea gas.

In a situation of the type described, a very satisfactory profit record may not necessarily indicate management strength (of course it certainly does not lead to the opposite conclusion). High past performance is therefore a useful indicator of management competence, but not a completely reliable one.

Failure to invest

It is often quite easy to make a company much more profitable for a year or two by not spending money on the maintenance of the resources of the business. In an extreme case, the development of new products is slowed down or stopped, only breakdown maintenance is carried out and plant is not replaced unless absolutely essential. In every possible way expenditure is deferred.

Stringent control of spending and disregard for investment in future business development can produce a profit spurt that may mask the underlying profit trend of a business. An examination of the company's profit and loss statement and balance sheets probably will not reveal what has been taking place and the profit trend may look very good indeed but, despite that, the company may be a bad investment.

Sometimes such practices arise, for example, because an elderly chief executive, who is also a major shareholder, has lost interest in growth and is content to let things just freewheel in his last few years in business. In other situations it is a deliberate practice in order to show satisfactory profit figures as an act of management self-preservation. It is sometimes done just to get a good selling price for a business.

Whatever the reason, a thorough appraisal is necessary in order to make sure that an apparently favourable profit trend is founded on a real improvement in underlying performance.

Practical situations

These are just a few of the circumstances in which the extrapolation of past trends could lead to an unreliable forecast. In practice such circumstances are far from rare.

Reliance on one product

One example is of a man who owned a business making wooden umbrella handles. He had started originally in a shed in his garden, but demand was high and business prospered. He acquired factory space, well-equipped with special-purpose machines, and with a labour force of about fifty machinists with all the necessary supporting services.

He was working to capacity, and obtaining additional investment funds in order to expand, when the first steel umbrella handles became available and, within a few years, his business was in liquidation. Here was a case when a study of the accounts would have shown a sound business, making an essential product with a steady growth in profits, good forward order book, low stocks and work-in-progress.

Hidden management change

Another example is of a company with a turnover of about $60 million making domestic appliances. The profit record had been patchy because it was affected by the cyclic quality of the market, but nevertheless each peak had been higher than the previous one and the general trend was upwards. The management could see that there was likely to be a series of mergers, and had already forecast that, in the end, there would only be five major manufacturers left in the industry. They believed that their company would be one of the five; based on their past performance in a difficult market this seemed highly likely. Then suddenly the Deputy Managing Director of the company died at a very young age. As far as the outside world was concerned the company had not changed at all; it had the same products, the same market; the management team was substantially the same, with the same Managing Director; and yet it had entered in a period of decline that could have been detected within the company.

The company started coasting rapidly downhill and within a very few years it had been absorbed by one of its competitors, and one for which, in its heyday, it would have had very little respect. The reason why this happened was that the Deputy Managing Director had been the real driving force in the company and it was he who held the rest of the management team together. The Managing Director, who was also Chairman of the company, although he had started the company, was an indecisive man and a poor leader.

Technological obsolescence

A third example is of a company producing capital plant that was acquired by a financial institution on behalf of its clients. The company has been in existence for about eight years and had increased its profits substantially for each of these years. The entrepreneur who had built the company had a very good technical idea which had allowed him to produce a better product than his competitors at a substantially cheaper price. The profit growth in the early years was due to a rapid market penetration, with plenty of profit margin available, so that he did not have to control the business particularly closely in order to make a profit.

His competitors began to develop products based on the same technology, but by the time they did so he was well established and at first, therefore, the competition caused him no serious problems. However, they were not content just to catch up; they had been shocked by being caught out with an inferior product and they were determined that it would not happen again. Mainly because of the lesson he had taught them, they were spending substantial amounts of money to develop newer, better products, whereas he, to maintain his profit record in the face of increasing competition, was spending almost nothing on product development.

When he realized that nemesis was not far away he agreed to sell his business at an attractive price to a very willing buyer. A year after the acquisition the company only broke even and the following year it lost about $1,350,000. What had happened was that a main competitor had introduced a new range of equipment which represented another product breakthrough.

Almost any financial appraisal of the company would have shown a good picture, stocks conservatively valued, rapid growth in turnover, declining but still very satisfactory margins, and total profit trend upwards. A market study would probably not have indicated that a new product was anticipated, or that it would be such an advance on existing products, although a really perceptive study might have shown that certain developments going on overseas posed a possible challenge. A deeper study of the company would, however, have indicated that inadequate resources were being expended on new product development and would certainly have revealed the absence of a properly supported forward long-term profit plan.

Summary

These are just a few illustrations of the weakness of inferring too much from the company's past achievements, or its present balance sheet. It is an important theme of this book that, although an examination of past trends is an essential step in the evaluation of profit potential, it supplies only one piece of information among the many which are needed to build up a picture of a company's probable future performance. Over-reliance on the projection of past trends has often led to disastrous results.

Chapter Three

IDENTIFYING STRENGTHS

Every individual has a unique set of characteristics that determine whether or not he will be good at specific sports or occupations and how he will react in a whole range of business and social situations. Similarly, every company has a distinctive set of characteristics which indicate directions of future development that are likely to be favourable.

Taking the analogy further, many individuals, either by accident or because their full potential has never been discovered, find themselves working in occupations far below their innate capacity. Historically it has probably always been true that the majority of people have been in this situation. Even today, people's expectations are conditioned by upbringing, education, environment, etc., so that they do not push themselves to the limit of their abilities and often never discover their real strengths or limitations.

The main point, however, is that no individual has completely rounded abilities. A man may be considered a great athlete, but he will not be good at both sprints and the marathon; a great artist is unlikely to be a great mathematician. Even in a single discipline, an outstanding theoretical physicist is generally not a good experimental physicist and vice versa. This is not because of lack of application in the relevant fields, but because the individual's fundamental aptitudes come into play.

The potential for success in any individual is thus related to specific fields of competence and will be realised only in activities where that competence is relevant. To achieve success it is usually necessary to build on strengths rather than try to remedy weaknesses; to find the opportunity for the man rather than reshape the man to the opportunity. There are exceptional individuals who overcome handicaps to become outstanding in a particular field; but usually the handicaps they overcome are secondary to the situation—a man with a speech defect may become a great orator, a man without exciting ideas never will.

Such considerations are equally true of companies. Each company has a unique history, product range, distribution system, manufacturing facilities and, above all, a unique group of people—the total effect of which is to provide a distinctive capability that can be employed to produce a profitable return. The profit opportunity must, however, be one that suits the specific capability of the business. There is no such thing as all-round competence, even though some conglomerate companies claim it in the form of management skill.

One difference between an individual and a company in this respect is that an individual's basic endowment is fixed, whereas a company in its history can undergo many metamorphoses. Such changes, however, take a considerable time and the chrysalis of a puss moth is unlikely to turn into a dragonfly.

Management myopia

A primary step in evaluating profit potential is therefore to find out what is the distinctive capability of the business. The managers of the business will, of course, have ideas about this which can form a very useful starting point for further study. Their views should not, however, be accepted at face value, because they sometimes turn out to be unreliable. Their viewpoint may well be coloured by the role they play within the business and hence by their preoccupation with specific performance factors. These factors may well be related to the capability of the business, but may not necessarily be distinctive.

For example, in almost every manufacturing company, managers would claim that high product quality is one of the strengths of the company. In comparative terms this self-evidently cannot be true. It is frequently considered to be true, because of the effort which must always be expended to maintain even reasonable levels of quality—'it takes a great deal of management effort and therefore the results must be good'—is the unspoken argument. Another reason for the frequency of this claim is that it is a manifestation of the tribal instinct 'ours is best'.

The fact is, however, that a strength the managers of the company believe to be present may not be there to the extent that it provides any competitive advantage. Similarly, managers may often receive most of their information about the marketplace through the company's own salesmen. The truth may then be distorted for a number of reasons, such as:

1 Salesmen tend to be temperamentally optimistic.
2 They will have a tendency to present in a good light their own part in the total marketing effort.
3 They, in turn, will get a picture from their customers who will naturally express views favourable to their own ends (prices are too high—for example).

Managers may thus get a misleading picture of their own company's performance and may therefore be unreliable informants on the fundamental reasons for its success.

Another factor that causes a distorted view of the situation is the effect of a company's history. A small company is formed and grows by exploiting its particular strengths in the market circumstances applying at the time. Years later, when the company is big and successful, the market circumstances may have completely changed, yet the memory of the great pioneering days may induce a belief that the skills and methods responsible for its early growth are the real source of the company's strengths and that the intensive application of these, today, will ensure a similar new growth phase.

In fact, of course, those strengths may be completely irrelevant to the current situation, because the markets will be different—'any colour you like as long as it is *not* black'—and because, as a company grows, its whole management style will have changed.

The management view of the company's strengths may often be distorted, therefore, by:

1 Limited information about what their competitors are providing in terms of service and products to the same market.
2 A tendency to take too favourable a view of what the company is doing because it is 'their' company.
3 Recollections of the determinants of past success.

Service versus product advantages

The managers of one profitable company manufacturing and marketing machine tools thought that they owed their success to particular technical advantages of their machines compared with the competitive products. In fact, a number of similar products were available, none of which were conclusively better or worse than their own. The particular feature of which they were so proud was only one feature among many and not decisive.

Their real advantage was that they provided an excellent spares service from stock, so that if a user had a breakdown he could almost certainly get a spare part within 24 hours. The dealers recognized this and therefore realized that if they recommended to their customers this company's machines they, in turn, would not have service problems in later years. Therefore, the crucial factor which gave them their competitive edge was the ready availability of spares.

The importance of recognizing this, is illustrated by the fact that the company wished to invest more funds in its research and development programme and was concerned about the amount of money tied up in stocks of spare parts. Management had decided to change their stockholding policy in respect of spares to release funds, on the grounds that none of their competitors found it necessary to give a 24 hour spares service, except on current models. Because of their mis-assessment of the source of their success, management were in danger of making a harmful change in policy.

Acquisition problems

When a company is being acquired it is absolutely crucial to find out as much as possible about its distinctive competence because it may be something that will cease to exist in its new environment.

Big, successful, but fairly staid companies often acquire young thrusting companies with the intention, for instance, of buying the new technology which appears to them to be the source of the acquired company's business success. They then find to their disappointment that, after acquisition, the success they were buying has somehow evaporated. This is often because the really important competence of the acquired company was not its technology but its highly flexible approach to its markets, which comes only from an entrepreneurial attitude to management and can soon disappear when it is constrained by the formalized systems of a large enterprise. In this situation, failure to recognize the source of the distinctive competence can lead to serious errors of management judgement.

There are situations in which a technical breakthrough is responsible for a company's success. If it is a fortuitous invention it may not recur, so it brings the company temporary success, but leaves it very vulnerable to the inroads of further technical developments. One manufacturer of mobile cranes had ten years of great success on such an invention, and then sold his business just when time was running out; the purchaser mistakenly thought that what he was buying was management flair, when in fact what he was buying was a brilliant design idea that was just losing its competitive edge.

Distinguishing factors

In searching for a company's distinctive competence it is not enough just to identify the strengths of the company. Some strengths may be developed to a very high degree and yet they may be largely irrelevant from the point of view of profit generation, or alternatively, they may be essential but not distinctive. In the evaluation of profit potential it is necessary to seek capabilities that are, in combination, unique, and which are directly related to the generation of profits.

For example, in the United Kingdom there is a relatively small number of large supermarket chains competing with each other. They all have large stores in main shopping areas, they all buy merchandise in bulk and sell it more cheaply than a typical small business. None of them offers its merchandise on average more cheaply than the others (at least not to a significant degree). They have, therefore, strengths which are essential to their mode of business, but as they each have the strengths to approximately the same degree, such strengths, although essential, cannot in themselves constitute the distinctive capability of each of the businesses in relation to the others. There are, of course, other factors operating which have led to differences in growth rate and differences in profitability. Factors such as:

1　Reputation for quality.
2　Reputation for low prices (not necessarily based on reality).
3　High standards of housekeeping and cleanliness.
4　Above average effectiveness in planning and control of stock.
5　Greater skills in site selection.
6　Astute selection of merchandise.

In this example the main strenths of the businesses are similar; the factors that made them distinctive and which have a major influence on their profitability appear, superficially, to be of second order of importance. This also highlights another aspect of the search to identify a company's distinctive capability. The distinguishing characteristics may apply at a number of levels. For example, one set of characteristics may distinguish a whole group of companies from the generality of companies in the same field of business; with an entirely different set of characteristics determining differential profitability within the group. In essence, therefore, it is the total combination of characteristics that uniquely determines a company's success. It may be built up from strength across the whole field of functional skills, or it may arise from particular excellence in a single aspect of the business. It may not be at all obvious to a superficial examination and this may even lead to a misleading conclusion.

Any evaluation of profit potential must therefore entail a study of a business as a whole and attempt to identify the relevant strengths in such matters as

1 Management balance and competence.
2 Marketing skills.
3 Distribution strengths.
4 Distinctiveness of the product or service.
5 Technical or craft skills.
6 Manufacturing capability and efficiency.
7 Effectiveness of financial control.

Such a systematic study will reveal factors which, in combination, represent the company's distinctive capability and this is the foundation of any assessment of profit potential.

Rate of change

To return to the comment that businesses are not fixed and immutable; the recent spate of companies engaged in tea or rubber planting, etc., that have been reshaped, renamed and then have emerged as dynamic investment companies, may make it appear that such changes can be accomplished easily. These are not typical, however, because these companies were needed only because they had a public quotation; their original content was intentionally discarded. In a normal situation, an attempt to develop a company into areas of business that require substantially different levels of competence is a time consuming and uncertain process. A very large amount of management effort can be expended with very little to show for it.

Of course diversification is possible. Companies are doing it successfully all the time. It is a primary aspect of new product development that, in the long term, diversification is an essential strategy for survival. Nevertheless, rapid diversification as a means of profit improvement is almost always unsuccessful if it entails the need for a significantly different business competence.

Identification of distinctive competence

It has been suggested earlier that managers may not correctly identify, in the first instance, the distinctive capability of their company. They do, however, have the collective knowledge which allows them to identify it. If a group of managers with different functional roles are brought together in discussion, then ideas soon emerge which, if subjected to rigorous questioning and discussion, will generally lead to a working definition.

During the course of an appraisal of profit potential, a much deeper study takes place in each of the functional areas and this study throws further light on the strengths and weaknesses of the business, and will confirm and extend the original definition, or cause it to be set aside in favour of an alternative view. In some cases, it may be necessary to carry out market studies before it is really possible to be sure that the correct definition has been reached; for example it is obviously significant to know why customers buy from the company and not from its competitors.

At times it may help for discussions in this field to be led by a third party who knows very little about the company initially and, therefore, has no preconceptions. Such an outside individual obviously cannot provide the answer, but he may often ask the vital questions that allow the management team themselves to reach a more satisfactory conclusion than would otherwise have been possible.

Summary

Every business has a unique collection of strengths which change relatively slowly. Profit growth must generally be built from those strengths. Therefore, evaluation of profit potential depends, in the first instance, on understanding what those strengths are and how they differ from those of competitors. The identification of such a distinctive competence is usually possible by objective questioning of the company's own management assumptions, supported by factual market knowledge.

Chapter Four

THE APPRAISAL

The profitability of a business depends on a very wide range of factors. The extent and quality of its resources are obviously of considerable relevance, but even more important is the skill of management in using those resources and in building up new resources in the fields of greatest profit opportunity.

Future profitability is therefore dependent not just on existing business trends, but on objectives, ideas, plans and policies. Some of these may have been explicitly formulated, while others may be in various stages of discussion. An assessment of profit potential must necessarily entail assumptions about such future policies.

The exploration of new markets, the development of new products and the introduction of new manufacturing methods are among the essential activities of any business. The company's plans in respect of these, and many other factors, have a crucial bearing on its profit performance. In a growth business, there will probably also be plans to expand by acquiring other businesses, which will entail the allocation of funds and other resources. Normally, there is the expectation that the rate of return on the acquired business will sufficiently augment the existing profitability, to improve the total percentage return.

Need for a corporate plan

Plans for change of any kind are highly relevant to the assessment of the profit potential of a business, and their effects certainly cannot be detected from observing past business trends. It is therefore not possible to evaluate profit potential without using some form of corporate plan.

Even the unmodified projection of an existing trend is based on the implied assumption that the market will go on behaving as it has done in the past, and that the company's marketing policies will be substantially unaltered, so that, even in this case, a corporate plan is implied, although no attempt has been made to define it.

In the case of companies which have a well established planning process, such a corporate plan will already be in existence, and in order to evaluate the profit potential the validity of the plan and the likelihood of its fulfilment must be examined. If a plan does not exist, then it is necessary to construct one as part of the evaluation process.

Fallibility of plans

A corporate plan is, however, only a paper exercise. It is possible, using apparently tenable assumptions, to construct a plan that will lead to almost any outcome. Much depends upon the optimism or pessimism with which the plan is prepared, or on how imaginative or practical are the individuals involved. Many companies produce forward plans which are carefully developed and have a satisfactory internal logic, yet are consistently very different from the actual profit achievement.

Figure 4.1 illustrates this. This was taken from the planning records of a small company making electronic equipment. There was a well developed corporate planning process that led to the publication of successive five-year plans for the business. In 1967, the five-year plan predicted that the 1972 profits would be £350,000. That forecast was steadily reduced each year until the current year budget predicted profits at only £200,000. The actual outcome was rather lower than this at £174,000.

Year plan issued	Planned profits, £'000				
	1968	1969	1970	1971	1972
1967	110	125	210	270	350
1968		125	160	204	265
1969			132	172	220
1970				145	200
1971					200
Actual	104	114	98	142	174

Figure 4.1   Comparison between planned and actual profits

In this example the achievement was consistently below the profitability indicated in the corporate plan. This is not an uncommon occurrence, which seems to arise because managers tend to assume that the factors favourable to their plans will predominate. They often fail to see, or ignore, unfavourable factors, or assume that they will somehow be overcome.

It is probably not unreasonable that managers should take an optimistic view and set objectives that are difficult to achieve, and it is natural that they would not aspire to mediocrity. In the evaluation of profit potential, however, it is necessary to take a dispassionate view and estimate the probability of achieving the plan. There is a well known law afflicting every human endeavour 'if things can go wrong, they will' to which some people would add 'and even if they couldn't possibly'. In the evaluation of profit potential it is important to consider even the things that could not possibly go wrong.

Success in implementing a corporate plan depends on the quality of management and other resources which are employed. Very good plans may fail because they are poorly implemented and, equally, plans that are fundamentally unsound may be carried through by skilled improvisation.

The evaluation of profit potential therefore calls for two complementary activities:

1 The establishment or validation of a profit plan.
2 An assessment of the company's capability of carrying out the plan with the resources available.

As it would obviously be meaningless to put down a plan known to be unachievable, the processes of building the plan and assessing its validity are normally carried out concurrently. So, to some extent, the two processes referred to above merge into each other. Nevertheless, as far as possible, it is better to think of the two aspects separately; it may be that a particular plan is technically feasible, but only if certain changes are made to the existing management situation, or product range, or market, etc. The conclusion might be, therefore, that the full potential of the company could be reached by taking certain actions, but that if these were not taken, then the profit potential would be reduced to a specified extent. Both plans and resources have therefore to be considered as being open to change.

Assessment of risk

An associated need is to form a view about the quality of the profit forecast. In the paragraphs above it was indicated that a company may fail to achieve its profit forecast because of optimism in forecasting or because of weaknesses in performance. There are situations, however, in which a forecast may be unreliable because of lack of basic information about important aspects of the business, without necessarily being too optimistic. The forecast is of low quality not because of any lack of care or judgement but because there is inadequate information to support it.

Obviously in a situation of this kind if the forecast return is relatively low there will be no point in considering investment at all, but if the forecast return is high it may be appropriate to accept the risk because of the high potential return.

Conceptually it is possible to consider an investment matrix as shown in Figure 4.2. In such a matrix, point A—high profit potential low risk, is what every businessman is searching for; point B—low profit potential high risk, is what many of them find instead; but probably the majority of investments will lie near to the diagonal line from the origin through point C, in the sense that high profit potential goes with high risk and it is not necessarily possible to reduce the latter without reducing the former.

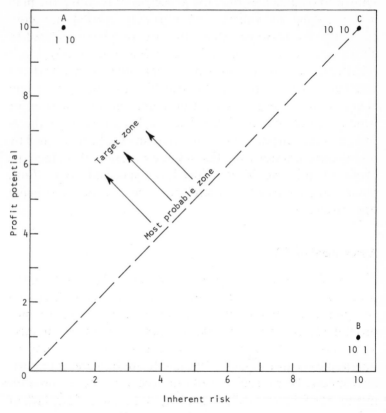

Figure 4.2   Profit potential/risk

The purpose in carrying out a detailed profit appraisal is to make sure that, as far as possible, resources are invested only in projects which would rank well to the left of the diagonal line in the matrix. However, although this matrix is useful in illustrating the risk/profit potential relationship it is not suggested that the matrix is a practical tool of measurement; the assessment of risk is usually a matter of informed judgement rather than of empirical measurement.

Method of carrying out an appraisal

The appraisal is concerned with factual information about the business, but there is also a need to look beyond the balance sheet at such matters as the plans for the future, the less tangible resources, the quality of management, and all the other factors which may influence business performance.

An appraisal of profit potential, whether of a whole business or just part of it, normally can be broken into four phases:

1 A study of the balance sheet, profit and loss statements and similar information, particularly including a study of the corporate plan for the business, if one exists.
2 Discussions with each key member of the management team in order to find out the ideas, relationships, problems and strengths of management.
3 Reference to basic information within the company as far as it throws further light on past performance or future plans.
4 The formulation of conclusions.

Examination of published date

An examination of the information published within a company is, therefore, the first step in getting to understand it. This would normally include:

1 Records of the past financial performance including the published profit and loss accounts and balance sheets, and management accounts where available.
2 If available, summaries of key management ratios, such as added value per employee, rate of turnover of stocks, ratios of debtors and creditors to turnover, etc.
3 Product catalogues, any available descriptive material on products, and similar publicity material.
4 Management organization chart and job specifications.

5 Any available statements and information concerning
business strategy and objectives.
6 Existing profit plans and budgets.

Every company will have its own range of information. After
studying what is available, further information should be
asked for in the form in which it is usually presented within the
business, rather than in a special format. Of course, it may be
more convenient to receive the information arranged in a way
that simplifies the analysis of the data; it may, therefore, be
tempting to ask the company's chief accountant to tabulate
certain information in a specified way. However, the form in
which information is available is often very revealing about a
company. For instance, the orderliness with which information is assembled, the facts which management think are
important enough to collate and analyse on a regular basis, are
informative about management thinking.

It is not, of course, the volume of management information
available which is of interest, but the quality of the information as a basis for management decisions. Some of the best
systems provide only two or three pages of information to each
manager each month, or even as little as a single page; but the
information has been so carefully selected that it gives him
good knowledge of the company's general situation and the
performance of his own department. Other companies provide
thirty or forty pages of management information which may
overload the recipient with detail.

In the latter situation it may be materially easier to carry out
an appraisal because such a large volume of data is available;
sorting the relevant from the irrelevant is not inconvenient for
a single investigation, but may be quite unsatisfactory to management as a regular routine.

It is generally true that if a very large volume of information
is available managers do not use it. This is one of the reasons
why computer print-outs are commonly filed away and
ignored—the volume is just too much for one man to assimilate.

There are companies in which there is no routine monthly
information, or a few disjointed analyses from which it is not

possible to form a comprehensive picture of the business. This can make the factual part of the appraisal difficult, and may indicate that the business is not being effectively controlled, or that management is non-numerate and therefore discounts the value of quantitative control data.

Discussions with managers

When the available published data has been thoroughly absorbed, the next phase is a series of discussions with key executives, at general management level and in each of the main functional fields, in order to form an assessment of the less tangible aspects of the management of the business. Later in this book, some very general questions are suggested in each of the fields of management. It is not, however, implied that the discussions should be tightly structured. Every business is different and no check list can possibly cover all possibilities. A manager should therefore have the opportunity, in discussion, to present his own views about the business and the factors that may influence its future profitability.

The purpose of having prepared questions is, therefore, only to act as a reminder that certain issues should be raised, and to stimulate discussion in the topics of greatest relevance to the problems of profit planning and forecasting. What is needed is a series of quite relaxed discussions which cover the fields that seem important to business performance, but which are by no means limited to such fields. If the manager concerned wishes to develop themes of his own, this will normally provide a far greater insight into his attitude to the business than would ever be provided by a question and answer session.

Basic information

During the discussions with managers it will become clear how much basic information is available within the business as a support for the profit plan, and how far the plan has been built on non-factual and perhaps mainly subjective considerations. It is obviously desirable to examine the supporting data and to draw conclusions about its validity and general value as support to the profit plan. It may be that, in order to complete the appraisal, additional information will have to be obtained.

This applies particularly in the marketing field. A reliable sales forecast is so important in profit planning that if this is in doubt then the whole plan is unsatisfactory. In order to have any confidence in a profit plan, it may therefore be necessary to study the company's markets in greater detail than has been its past practice.

Company acquisition

If the evaluation is being carried out with a view to the acquisition of the business, there is some change of emphasis. For example, the acquirer may be intending to change the use of some of the company's resources; or the business may be being purchased from a retiring owner and so there may be a need for a new management team. Nevertheless, the principles above still apply except that it is the plans of the future owner that have to be quantified, and the capability of the new management team evaluated. This can be much more difficult, because the plans are likely to be far more general in nature, and the management without experience in that particular situation. Nevertheless, the fact that any form of discontinuity, such as new ownership or new management, makes it more difficult to evaluate profit potential, does not remove the necessity to make such an evaluation in the most logical and objective way possible.

Forming conclusions

The information obtained during each of the three phases —the study of published data, discussions with management, the study of basic information—should normally provide a consistent pattern which will enable conclusions about the future profitability to be drawn. If a profit plan is not available, then it is necessary to prepare one based on the information gained during the study and, depending on the purpose of the appraisal, probably get management agreement to such a profit plan.

If a consistent pattern does not emerge, then essential factors have probably been missed and there is a need for a further study to eliminate the inconsistencies.

Summary

An appraisal of the profit potential of a business is normally carried out by first examining a selection of the available information about the company, particularly including the profit plan. Then there should be a series of informal discussions, with key executives, carried out in a relaxed, informal way. The supporting information behind the profit plan should be examined and evaluated, then from all the information, both quantitative and qualitative, a judgement can be formed about the profit potential of the business.

Chapter Five

THE PROFIT PLAN

As was indicated in the previous chapter, the evaluation of profit potential is not possible without a corporate plan. The plan may be one which merely assumes that the company will continue in its present line of business or it may entail major policy changes. The former case is the easier to evaluate because there are no discontinuities; the trends under study already exist and it is a matter of judging their future rate of change.

If a business is embarking on a major programme of diversification, perhaps by acquisition of other businesses, then the corporate plan will almost certainly include an appreciable amount of contingency planning which will make assessment difficult. In such a situation it will be almost certainly an assessment of management which will play a primary part in reaching conclusions.

Most companies fall between these two extremes in that an appreciable proportion of their future growth is expected to be derived from improvement in performance in existing fields of business, and a rather smaller proportion from diversification or radical change.

In every case there is a need for a profit plan that delineates the main assumptions on which the company's growth is planned, and which derives profit forecasts from those assumptions.

Existing profit plan

If the company has a profit plan already and if that plan is available for examination and questioning, then the problems of quantifying the profit potential of the business are substantially simplified. The plan will necessarily depend on certain assumptions about the behaviour of the market, about the changes in economic conditions, about probable responses of competitors, customer purchasing habits, new product development, and investment in new products and processes; which, as assumptions, can be examined individually.

In examining the validity of these assumptions it is possible to refer to the evidence on which they were originally founded, and it is also possible to obtain new information which may or may not provide them with support. Normally it will be found that some of the assumptions are well based and beyond serious dispute, others will be found to be matters of reasonable judgement but difficult to substantiate in precise terms, and some of the assumptions will have been made without serious thought and may not be based on any worthwhile evidence.

The latter situation arises usually because businesses, like other institutions, tend to develop their own culture which may accept certain concepts as being absolute when, in fact, they are only a distillation of limited experience. For example, a company which has grown very successfully from small beginnings by the adoption of a very competitive pricing policy, may hold as a self-evident truth that 'if prices are reduced, turnover will increase, and so will profitability'. This may have been true for a company selling to less than one per cent of the market and aspiring to double or treble its turnover; but it would be less likely to be true of a company holding 20 to 30 per cent of a market and attempting to take another 10 per cent. There are many similar examples of attitudes, which were very appropriate to a smaller struggling company, that become part of the accepted folklore just at a time when the company has grown beyond the stage when they were relevant.

A basic requirement, therefore, is to examine each of the basic assumptions that underlie a profit plan, and to challenge those that appear to have inadequate evidential support.

This is not to say that any business plan can be completely objective in its foundations; it is not possible to obtain all the facts applying to any situation. What matters is that the weight of evidence should support any given assumption and that there should be sufficient of it. The use of the word 'sufficient' introduces a subjective consideration, which is why the evaluation of profit potential always depends on experience and judgement as well as systematic analysis.

If there is already a profit plan, the first stage in the evaluation of profit potential is to obtain a deep understanding of the underlying assumptions which support the plan and to make sure that it is free from internal inconsistencies.

Building a profit plan

If the company does not have a profit plan already, or if the plan is found to be based on shifting sand, then it is necessary to build a profit plan from first principles as part of the evaluation process. Normally, the information required would be obtained from the executives responsible for day-to-day management of the business functions concerned. Their ability to produce the data is of considerable interest in forming judgements about the ability of the management team.

While the plans are being prepared, the company's distinctive competence is used as a reference point; it determines the kinds of markets the company can successfully enter, its capability of producing the right products for those markets, the effectiveness with which it can manufacture or supply the products. In essence it limits the range of strategies open to the business, but also clarifies the opportunities available.

It is necessary therefore to decide, in the light of the identified distinctive competence what is the appropriate strategy for the business, and then to quantify the likely outcome of following such a strategy. It may be that there is more than one attractive strategy, and it may be desirable to produce, at least in outline, more than one set of plans in order to predict the likely outcome of making separate choices.

It is never possible, however, to get sufficient information to make an entirely objective choice between alternative courses. In the end it is necessary to make a subjective judgement based on the best available evidence. To seek an absolute standard of assessment is to fail to make an assessment at all, or to vascillate between choices as each additional piece of information is produced. On the whole, therefore, it is necessary to assemble a reasonable amount of information, but to be aware of the effect of the law of diminishing returns.

There is another circumstance in which it may be necessary to prepare more than one forecast, that is when a company is planning an expansion programme from limited financial resources, and it is necessary to explore the effect of this constraint. This may not only affect how far a company can go down a particular development path, but it may make a great deal of difference between the attractiveness of various business strategies.

Sales forecast

Quantification of future profit potential starts with the examination of the company's sales forecast, which must be based on forecasts of the future turnover for each main product group and for each market. This would necessarily be subdivided in fine detail for the first year and in decreasing detail for subsequent years. Normally, for companies with a relatively short (up to two year) product development cycle, a five-year sales forecast is the best that can be expected for profit planning purposes, although longer term information may give general support to the trend. For companies with very long product development or manufacturing cycles, it may be necessary to extend the planning period to ten years or longer. These companies are the exception rather than the rule and for most companies five years is adequate.

The degree of subdivision of the profit forecast depends very much on the products concerned. As far as it is possible to generalize, every market that has characteristics differing from others to the extent that it requires a distinct product range, should be separated in the plan. For example, a company manufacturing industrial boilers may sell some boilers for steam-raising, some for heating water and some for process heating. In a sales forecast these will obviously be separated because their markets would be affected by different external factors and therefore would potentially experience different rates of change.

The forecast should also separate those markets dealt with by different selling and distribution patterns. A company selling consumer products to small retailers under its own brand name and to supermarkets under their brand names, would obviously separate these in a sales forecast used for profit planning purposes. A similar consideration would apply to the separation of sales to various export markets.

A third general division, largely for later convenience of reporting, is that items which are likely to be manufactured in different factories, on different assembly lines, or by different processes, should, if possible, be separated in the sales forecast. A manufacturer of communications equipment, for example, would naturally require separate forecasts for frequency-modulated and amplitude-modulated equipment, in order to take account of the limiting effect of testing capacity.

Each of the above subdivisions of the sales forecast will create difficulties for forecasters, but it will also make forecast more precise and more usable. Precision comes by considering each of the market subdivisions separately and examining the trends that affect those particular markets, which can include:

1 Population changes.
2 Long-term shifts in market demand.
3 New product developments.
4 Obsolescence of individual products.
5 New marketing initiatives.
6 Competitive initiatives.
7 The decline of competitive activities.
8 Changing selling performance.

By considering each of the influences separately, and by carefully considering the negative as well as the positive factors, it is possible to form a reasonable assessment of likely future sales levels. It is important that the sales forecast be built up in this way from the external market data by the means most appropriate to the particular company and market. Generalized forecasts are by definition unacceptable for the purpose of assessing profit potential.

Sales forecasting is, however, a complex topic, and the detailed techniques are beyond the scope of this book. A very useful summary is given in *Market and Sales Forecasting* by Gordon Bolt.

Selling costs

As the sales forecast is being developed, the methods of marketing will be established; this makes it possible to estimate the cost of each aspect of marketing. Most of the normal costs such as salaries, travel expenses, sales office overheads, and similar items, are relatively easy to estimate with reasonable accuracy. Other items such as advertizing costs and discount allowances may be more difficult to estimate.

The effectiveness of advertizing is not easily measurable in most business situations; it is only in the high volume consumer goods market that there is reasonable correlation between advertizing expenditure and changes in the business volume. The effect of advertizing is generally hard to predict, and it may be necessary to explore past records in considerable detail to form a judgement about the extent of advertizing necessary in order to sustain a given volume. Where advertizing is relatively unimportant in the marketing mix, (as it may be for certain capital goods for instance) there is, in some companies, a tendency to use advertizing as the overhead regulator, cutting it back when times are hard, and increasing it when the turnover and profit situation is more satisfactory. This is obviously an illogical process and it is desirable that advertizing is adequately provided for in a profit plan.

For several reasons, discounts are a source of problems in forecasting selling costs. In many companies the discount structure is not systematically defined, but based on response to pressures from individual customers. Where this is the case the cost of discounts depends on which particular customers place orders in the given period.

If the sales department has discretion to grant discounts, then when orders are hard to get discount levels will tend to increase. This is particularly true if there is otherwise tight control on prices.

If, by contrast, the system of allocating discounts is strictly related to specific factors such as order size or total volume, then the cost is more likely to vary in a predictable way with sales turnover.

A careful examination of the way in which discounts are granted is therefore necessary in building the profit plan.

Manufacturing programme

If the company manufactures its own profits, the manufacturing programme is derived from the sales forecast. It may not be possible or desirable that the production rate should mirror closely the anticipated rate of order intake. For products that have a high rate of seasonal variability, for example, it may be quite impossible to manufacture at the peak rate, and unacceptable even if possible, to lay off workers to reduce output in the low season. It may therefore be desirable to produce for stock during the season of low demand. One other possibility is to adjust the promised delivery period, to extend delivery in periods of high demand and shorten it as demand falls. This is obviously an economical way of dealing with the situation from the company viewpoint, but it may well be unacceptable in the market-place.

Usually, when the forecast sales demand is very variable, the production plan is based on a compromise; in the season of greatest demand, some additional output is achieved by overtime working and by employing additional operatives, some stock is made in advance and there is a limited extension of the normal delivery period.

In the case of an upward market trend rather than a seasonal variation, a similar situation applies. The production programme can rarely follow precisely the market forecast and so there is an approximate fit which relies on building up stocks at certain stages. There will, in such cases, be a requirement for capital to finance the necessary stocks.

When a satisfactory compromise has been reached, and the production programme has been decided, then material and labour costs can be assessed for each product group and the requirements for plant, factory space, and other physical resources can be evaluated. A total labour and material budget can then be established, as can the costs of the fixed and variable factory overheads necessary to produce the required output.

Product development

From the sales forecast and past records of the business it will usually be possible to estimate the likely life cycle of the products currently being produced. If the predicted turnover from those products is shown on a graph, the result will probably resemble the lower curve shown on Figure 5.1 where the turnover rises initially, then reaches a peak and begins to decline. The upper line on the same graph, which is the total sales forecast, can be reached only by developing new products to replace and supplement the existing ones; the difference between the two lines is the gap which must be filled by new product development.

The amount of development effort required to do this will depend on the average development time and cost for typical products, and also on the average life cycle of the products once they have been developed. These factors can be determined from the company's past history; it is therefore possible to deduce the extent of the resources which must be applied to new product development in order to make sure the gap is filled. From this examination it is then possible to calculate the operating costs of the development department and the likely requirement for all resources.

If the company is providing a service rather than a product, much the same considerations apply. From the sales forecast it is possible to calculate the levels of service that must be provided and, therefore, the costs of providing those services and the necessary rate of establishment of new services (because services like products usually have only a limited life cycle).

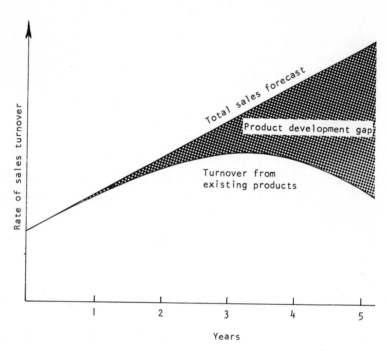

Figure 5.1   Product development gap

General overheads

When the marketing, manufacturing and product development requirements have been evaluated in terms of revenue, direct cost, fixed and variable overhead costs and capital requirements, the requirement for administrative support services such as personnel and financial management can be estimated. These are generally dominated by fixed costs, or costs which vary directly with the other components of the forecast; so they are not normally difficult to estimate, or subject to many unexpected variations.

Profit forecast

All the earlier forecasts can then be combined to form a profit forecast. This may show a profit level which is regarded as adequate; if it does not do so then management will almost certainly re-examine each part of the forecast in order to amend the figures to produce a more satisfactory forecast outcome.

From the viewpoint of the evaluation of profit potential this is obviously a matter of some importance because if the forecast was originally grounded on the best available information, it should not be possible to change it without radical changes in policy.

Cash flow

In each of the functional areas it is necessary to estimate the amount of capital required for additional fixed assets and also the funds which will be tied up in stocks, work-in-progress, debtors, and other elements of the working capital of the business.

This capital forecast, combined with the profit and loss forecast, makes it possible to prepare the cash flow forecast. This may indicate that the envisaged growth can be self-financing. On the other hand it may show that additional resources will be required; in which case it must be decided how the funds can be obtained and what they will cost, so that the cost can be included in the profit forecast.

Content of plan

As a minimum, a profit plan normally includes:

1 A sales forecast by individual market and product groups.
2 A forecast of selling costs.
3 A manufacturing programme and forecast of labour material and other variable costs.
4 A forecast of factory overhead costs.
5 An assessment of new product requirements.
6 A budget for the cost of developing the new products.
7 A forecast of the costs of the various supporting services.
8 A capital budget.

These are summarized to provide:

1 Profit forecast.
2 Capital requirement forecast.
3 Cash flow forecast.

Although, in the discussion above, a sequential programme has been suggested, in practice it is not as simple as that. There is an appreciable amount of feedback from one plan to another, for example the marketing plan must take account of the company's new product development capability and of products already under development. Equally it must be affected by the company's manufacturing capability and the speed with which new manufacturing resources can be developed. There are many interactions of this kind, so although forecasting generally starts with the market-place and continues in a logical sequence, in detail the process is a reiterative one with interaction and feedbacks between the various stages of building the plan.

Summary

Quantification of a company's profit plans entails an assessment of the probable changes in the environment in which the company is operating, and an assessment of the effect of applying the company's distinctive strengths to that environment under certain assumed and specified financial circumstances. There may be a choice of paths for the company's future and for each of them there will be high and low estimates of performance.

Chapter Six

PROBABILITY OF ACHIEVEMENT

It is not difficult to write a profit plan that shows a satisfactory rate of profit growth; achieving the results in practice can be a different matter.

A company's long-term plans may indicate that a satisfactory product performance is possible. The market forecast may appear to be well-grounded, the envisaged manufacturing and product development plans may be feasible, and the plans may have a satisfactory internal logic; yet there may be a significant shortfall in actual achievement. Such circumstances are too widespread to need much elaboration here. Every working manager will have known situations in which apparently well-founded plans have not been brought to successful fruition.

The cause for failure may be that the basic assumptions on which the plans were based were invalid; the market assessments were wrong for example, or planned reductions in product cost could not be achieved due to labour difficulties or inflationary pressures, or a new product failed to perform to specification or proved unreliable in service; perhaps the forecast was just over-optimistic.

It may be that the assumptions were basically correct, but that the deductions made from them proved to be invalid. For example, a company may correctly predict that, with the increase in public concern over environmental pollution, there is a good market for equipment to facilitate the disposal of domestic waste. The company, however, may then produce what turns out to be in market terms the wrong solution to the problem; for example it may develop an efficient incinerator with effective control of smoke emission, only to find that another manufacturer has developed a different process with greater emphasis on recovery of useful materials or energy. In such a situation, although the basic assumptions behind the company strategy were correct, the strategy derived from those assumptions turned out to be mistaken.

A third possibility exists when the assumptions are fundamentally correct and the strategy is correctly deduced from them, but there is weakness in the quality of execution. Any forward plan will call for changes in a company's way of working. It will need to develop new product ranges, change its methods of marketing, take on new agents, develop new distribution methods, etc.; its organization will have to be changed in order to carry out effectively the new tasks; new facilities will need to be planned and installed. The outcome of all these activities is dependent not just on the quality of the plan, but also upon the quality of execution.

The ability to implement a corporate plan successfully depends on the management strengths within the company. The required strengths include:

1 Ability to prepare interlocking detailed plans.
2 Skill in monitoring performance against such plans.
3 Ability to overcome the resistance which will inevitably arise if there is any major departure from existing practices.
4 Judgement about the pace of change that can be achieved in an organization.
5 Determination that the plans will be achieved whatever obstacles arise; but flexibility to modify plans if their basis proves to be wrong.

Detailed planning

Major plans are necessarily couched in general terms. Usually an appreciable amount of information has been obtained to support a decision to adopt a business strategy, which makes it seem advantageous. When the decision is made, the time of execution is usually fairly remote and the problems of implementation may easily be brushed aside as being matters of detail.

It is when the detailed planning starts that the difficulties emerge. Broad concepts then have to be translated into plans which affect individual people, entail the expenditure of specific sums of money and require judgements that are not at all as clear-cut as the original concept seemed to be.

For example, the board of directors of a manufacturing business may decide to close one of its factories and move the plant to another factory, perhaps taking advantage of economies of space arising from more efficient processes. It can be shown that there is space available in one factory for all the necessary output; it may be very easy to calculate how much money will be saved by closing one of the two factories; the choice between them may be an obvious one; perhaps only one is big enough for the combined output, or there may be differences in labour availability in the two areas. The major decision is therefore easy to take.

The detailed planning may, however, be relatively difficult. The move will obviously take several months. During that period customers must continue to be supplied. This may mean sub-contracting during the period of the move; but sub-contractors, if they can obtain business elsewhere, may be reluctant to undertake such work knowing it to be of limited duration. They may not therefore be very reliable suppliers. If the plant provides a service rather than a product, it may not be possible to sub-contract. The alternative to sub-contracting is probably to stockpile products prior to the move, but this may be equally difficult because of the problem of estimating the market demand during the period of the move.

Then comes the problem of what plant should be moved. Unless the product mix is fixed there is usually a choice depending on judgement about likely demand. If the plant is complicated, there will be modifications necessary both to facilitate the move and to make the plant more effective when it is re-installed. The period of the move may be the only opportunity to make modifications economically, so that there is a difficult decision: whether to risk delay and carry out the modifications, or to re-instal the plant as it is, knowing that another opportunity to make the necessary improvements will not come for many years.

Then there will be the most difficult question of all: how many people are to be offered jobs in the combined facility, what will happen to those for whom no jobs are available, what will be the basis of selection?

In a move of this kind, which may be shown to be logical for the business, there will be many thousands of individual decisions, a substantial proportion of which will depend not on objective calculation of benefits, but on finely balanced judgement between alternative courses of action, often with totally inadequate information. These decisions usually have to be made urgently in order not to delay the main programme of change. It is their quality which is so influential in controlling the success of the project.

There is no way in which all these decisions can be made in advance or monitored by some central authority. It is, however, possible by careful detailed planning of every aspect of a business to foresee some of the difficulties that may arise and to take the appropriate decisions before they become urgent, and therefore improve the probability of successful implementation of the general strategy. The quality of the detailed planning processes is therefore an important determinant of success in applying any business policy.

Monitoring and control

When plans have been made and changes put in hand, there is a need to monitor closely, on a systematic basis, what is happening to make sure the plans are being met and to take action to correct departures from them. Skill in deciding what should be monitored and in taking the right corrective action is important. To try to monitor everything, is to invite failure due to the weight of detail.

The common practice of applying inadequate pressure at the beginning of a project, building up to a major panic at the end, is also obviously unsatisfactory. Management judgement is needed about the degree of control necessary.

Overcoming resistance

There will always be resistance to the implementation of any plan entailing change. Much of the resistance will be due to feelings of insecurity engendered by the change, and some of the people affected may have good reason to feel insecure. Others will realize that an alternative course of action would offer them better opportunities and will, therefore, be trying to influence the company in the direction more favourable to them.

Apart from such personal considerations, there will be genuine differences of view about what is objectively best for the company. It is never possible to achieve the optimum solution for every individual department, and at the same time achieve the optimum solution for the business as a whole. There will, therefore, be some departments in which a planned change will have an adverse effect. Members of such departments will have real evidence that the change is harmful and good reason to oppose it.

Resistance to change, therefore, can arise from a variety of reasons, some of which are based on personal considerations and some on real concern for the business. Such objections must be overcome as constructively as possible. A manager with enough power and energy may perhaps just bulldoze his way through, but if things do not work out as planned he can expect very little help from the other people involved. A skilled manager will succeed by discussion and persuasion and will rarely find it necessary to use the sanctions of his authority. He will therefore tend to get more commitment from the other managers concerned.

Flexibility

Determination to achieve the required result, regardless of problems from any source, is obviously one of the key characteristics leading to success. If, however, circumstances do change, or the original assumptions are found to be faulty, then dogmatic insistence on following the original course is a frequent cause of business problems. There is a narrow path between on the one hand changing course every time there is the slightest indication that an external trend is changing, and on the other hand being unwilling to change plans even when the evidence for change is quite clear. To be too rigid about plans, or to be too flexible, can be equally harmful; it takes high quality judgement to avoid either of these extremes.

Pace of change

The rate of change that can successfully be achieved in any organization is relatively slow. There is a need first to get general acceptance of the necessity for the change, or at least a commitment to make it work. It is never possible to convince all the people involved, but at least each of the ones who has a key part to play in the change must be committed. This can entail a considerable amount of discussion and persuasion.

There is a need to retrain all the people involved and to make sure that they know what the changed way of working will entail. New organizational links will have to be formed and new personal relationships established as a consequence. The changes will not work entirely as planned, and it will be necessary to modify certain plans and possibly institute further changes in job specifications and organization.

Then, when the changes are fully introduced, they have to become part of the culture of the business, accepted by the majority of the people involved as an established way of operating which is fully understood. These factors apply to a greater or lesser degree whatever the change. The more important the change, then the longer is the period between initial discussion and the final acceptance as a normal practice.

If one change follows another too quickly, a normal pattern of working has no time to form before it is broken down and replaced by another one; in such circumstances managers, particularly in the lower management levels, may become disorientated and not able to assimilate the changes themselves or train their subordinates while still trying to carry on their normal work routines.

There is another danger of very rapid change. In every business there are informal ways of making the organization work which may have nothing to do with the formal management systems. Even the most highly organized businesses have such informal arrangements, but the weaker the formal systems the more the informal ones take over. Changes may break down such informal systems without providing an adequate replacement, and such a breakdown can have serious consequences for the short-term performance of the business.

For reasons of this kind too high a rate of change, however logically desirable, may cause performance to decline rather than improve. A profit plan that calls for rapid change in any aspect of business should therefore be treated with some reserve unless the management team is unusually talented and has shown ability to achieve similar rates of change in the past.

Management competence

The really crucial factor in all matters affecting the achievement of a planned profit level is the quality of management. It is the competence, decisiveness, leadership and flexibility of the company's managers, and their ability to work together as a team, that really decides whether the company's plans will be successfully executed. The assessment of management is therefore central to the evaluation of profit potential.

This will be partly based on a judgement about the calibre of managers involved compared with the generality of managers employed in similar situations throughout industry and partly on a study of how well they have performed before in meeting requirements similar to those inherent in the company's plan.

For example, if the plan calls for development of a new range of products, it is possible to consider the general qualifications and experience of the manager responsible for new product development, to evaluate the resources he has at his disposal, and to compare those with the probable needs of the situation. It is also possible to find out from company records such matters as:

1 The rate at which new products have been developed in the past.
2 The ratio of successful to unsuccessful products.
3 The length of a typical development cycle.
4 The proportion of the current turnover based on products which have been developed during specified periods in the past.

In this way a judgement can be formed about the probability of a current plan being achieved using the resources available.

In other fields of management it is also usually possible to find evidence of past rates of achievement and, therefore, to make deductions about the capability of the management team of achieving future change.

Of course, if there have been significant changes in management personnel, then it is not possible to make reliable deductions from past performance within the company concerned, although sometimes consideration of the relevant managers' achievements elsewhere may help in the evaluation of their calibre.

A manager who is intelligent and a capable organiser will often succeed in a diverse range of business situations, so that experience in a different situation is a good guide, provided that it calls for much the same personal qualities. As an example, a manager who has successfully managed a factory manufacturing machine tools in small batch quantities, is quite likely to succeed in managing a factory that mass-produces furniture. The technical content of the two jobs is different as are the problems of planning and control, but the personal attitudes that lead to success in one job will lead to it equally in the other. If the same manager attempts the transition, not to a completely different industry but to a sales role within his own industry, then he may well be unsuccessful because different personal qualities are called for.

This differentiation between the content of a job and its personal demands is important. A change in job content is easily assimilated, a change in personal demands may not be. Therefore, in considering a manager's total range of experience, the kinds of change are at least as important as their total extent.

Summary

The achievement of profit growth depends on resources, planning and execution. Of these the latter is the most difficult to assess. It depends heavily on the competence of the company's managers and their capability of working together as a team. Their specific past performance compared with that required in a profit plan is the most useful indicator of their capability of achieving the required results.

Chapter Seven

MANAGEMENT COMPETENCE AND STYLE

The most important source of strength (or weakness) of any business is the quality of its management team. The evidence for making such a statement is the marked difference in performance between companies of similar size operating in the same industry, or in the change that takes place in a company as a consequence of changes at top management level. Certainly, it is quality of management that determines how well based the company's profit plan is and how effectively it will be executed.

As was indicated in the previous chapter, a profit plan is built on a limited number of facts and a considerable amount of judgement. Normally the judgement will be made by the executives concerned with the relevant functional areas. In evaluating the plan it is obviously necessary to know whether they have sufficient depth of experience to form a valid judgement, and also to consider whether they are temperamentally likely to make a balanced judgement. If it is known that an executive is temperamentally optimistic or pessimistic it is relatively easy to take this into account, but some very capable executives have cyclic personalities and are subject to mood swings that may affect their judgement in an unpredictable way. This is not frequent perhaps, but it does arise often enough to make it necessary to think seriously about the stability of judgement of any executive involved in building a profit forecast.

When the plan is made there is the question of execution. As was indicated in Chapter Six it is relatively easy to take such big decisions as, for instance, to build a new factory in a low labour cost area, or to plan a new product range in order to enter a new market segment. During the implementation of such major decisions, however, there are many thousands of individual small decisions, and actions of various kinds, which determine whether or not each major decision will produce a satisfactory outcome.

Each of these small decisions is taken by an individual manager, probably in consultation with his colleagues; the quality of the decisions depend on the quality of management.

Some of the basic assumptions on which the profit plan was founded will turn out to be wrong. Competitors will not behave as predicted; they will introduce unexpected new products, reduce their prices, improve their service and generally behave in ways quite destructive to the company's own market position. There will be labour and material shortages and, at some stage, interest rates will change and capital will become difficult to get.

There will, of course, be favourable changes as well, but because of the general tendency of most managers to forecast optimistically, it is the unfavourable ones that will predominate and provide the real test of management competence.

It is necessary, therefore, to judge how effectively the managers will react to external changes, compensate for their effects, and bring the company back to its planned course. As was indicated earlier, the most useful guide to this is past performance, e.g. how well earlier profit plans have been met. Obviously a pattern of missed forecasts will cast considerable doubt on the management's ability to meet any current plans.

Leadership

In all the aspects of management competence, the quality of leadership of the management team is important. Effective

leadership holds the team together and makes sure that un-
avoidable conflicts are resolved constructively; it also provides
the driving force in achieving objectives. The ability and personality of the chief executive is by far the most important
single factor affecting business performance.

The qualities for the leadership role are particularly difficult
to define because there are so many different ways of leading.
However, as far as it is possible to generalize, essential qualities appear to be integrity, energy and the kind of intelligence
that takes pleasure in recognition and development of order,
rather than the analysis of detail.

In this sense the use of the word 'integrity' means not only
readiness to honour written, and much more important, un-
written obligations, but also a willingness to look at a given
situation with objectivity and make a decision which is, as far
as possible, not influenced by personal interest.

Another important factor in the leadership role is a reputation for success. This seems to work both on the leader him-
self, who becomes more willing to be adventurous in his
decision-making, and on the rest of the management team,
who are likely to co-operate more wholeheartedly with a man
who has such a reputation. Past success is, therefore, obviously
important in assessing leadership ability.

The charismatic type of leadership is probably not important in an industrial situation. A man's immediate colleagues
are likely to see him as he is and judge him by what he does, not
by the image he presents.

Management style

As indicated, there are many successful styles of management.
It is certainly not possible to say, particularly in this context,
that some of them are right and others are wrong. What can be
said with confidence is that differing styles may not mix easily
and if an attempt is made to do so, crises will almost certainly
ensue. One obvious example of this is when a chief executive
who has encouraged participation by his subordinates in management decisions, is replaced by one who has a more autocratic approach. In a situation such as this, problems are bound to

arise and almost certainly key individuals in the management team will leave. The degree of participation in management decision-making is therefore a matter to be explored.

Similarly, in some companies there is a good deal of personal interplay in arriving at decisions; in other companies, with an equal amount of participation in decision, the process is much more intellectual and less personalized.

The form of control is another indicator of management style. The chief executive may be a man who regularly visits all parts of his enterprise and personally observes what goes on there. He may rely heavily on his own observation and judgement. At the other extreme, the chief executive may rarely move away from his office and may rely on a reporting system to keep him informed about the company's circumstances. If there is a reporting system, the amount of detail and the emphasis on various aspects of performance also affect the perception of the individual executives about the management of the company.

The particular functional expertise of the chief executive is also relevant. Most men in such a role have spent a majority of their working life exercising a particular functional skill, which means they will probably be familiar with one particular aspect of the business in great depth and understand the others to a lesser degree. They will naturally be able to make a better contribution, but also be liable to interfere more, in the field in which they have greatest expertise. The managers of a company that has been led by a man who is predominantly a marketing specialist, and which is then taken over by another company where close financial control is the guiding principle, may feel disorientated by the change in management attitude.

There are many other aspects of management style that will emerge in the course of a study, all of which may influence the success of the business, particularly if an acquisition or merger is in prospect.

Basic requirements

In summary, therefore, whether or not a company will produce valid profit plans and then successfully carry them out closely depends on the calibre and balance of its management team. In assessing profit potential, evaluation of the management team is a primary consideration.

In the ideal situation:

1 Each member of the team is well qualified in the disciplines relevant to his specific responsibilities and has a working knowledge of those of his colleagues.
2 There is diversity of experience.
3 There is a balanced range of ages.
4 The managers work together as a team and are well led.

If all these needs are satisfied there is a high probability that the management team will be able to implement its plans effectively. On the other hand, if there are serious weaknesses in the areas indicated, then it is probable that optimum profitability will not be achieved.

Exploratory questions

After the primary documentary material has been studied, the next stage in an evaluation of profit potential is a study of management competence and style. A number of open-ended questions need to be asked; the answers, together with subsequent discussion to illuminate them, form a basis for the assessment of management.

Is the management team well balanced in terms of basic training and experience?

It is usually an unhealthy sign if too many of a company's management team have a similar background. If a majority come from a single management function, for example if the management team is dominated by salesmen or accountants or engineers, this can easily lead to distorted understanding of the constraints and opportunities influencing the company's policies. This is no criticism of the individuals involved. To be able to recognize an opportunity is, in part, a matter of having the right mental attitude, but it also requires an appropriate background of experience. Systematic analysis may be necessary to exploit an opportunity, but analysis will not necessarily lead to the opportunity being recognized initially. Normally, people are attuned to opportunities within their own fields of experience, but not to those outside such fields. In a company dominated by salesmen, for instance, there is likely to be ready identification of new marketing possibilities, but a blindness to the opportunities for technical innovation. In the reverse situation engineers may produce technical masterpieces for which there is no market demand.

There are also very real personality differences between successful salesmen, accountants, etc., which can colour their attitude to various management decisions. It is, therefore, quite important to have each of the main management disciplines represented in any top management team.

A common occurrence is for all the managers to have been promoted from within the company, or from within a group of companies. Any form of organizational inbreeding like this usually means that both strengths and weaknesses are accentuated. It is obviously harmful if all important management posts are filled from outside the company, but it can be equally harmful if none or very few are.

Problem-solving and identification of opportunities appear to be carried out most effectively when there is a diversity of experience contributing ideas. In discussion, individuals who challenge the accepted view or, through ignorance, ask 'stupid' questions can often trigger the process that leads to a solution. If the individuals involved have a similar background this is much less likely to take place. On the whole, therefore, diversity of experience is a healthy indicator.

Is the age range of the management team well distributed?

Young men are usually eager to make changes in the established way of doing things, and may be a powerful source of creative energy. They are sometimes idealistic and will often set themselves challenging objectives and then go to great lengths to meet them. Often, however, through lack of experience, they will fail to see all the implications of their ideas and so may adopt policies that have harmful effects which are not immediately obvious. They may also push other people faster than they are capable of moving. In that case the result may well be, not beneficial change, but serious disruption.

Perhaps the biggest risk is that they may not yet have reached, even for themselves, the right balance between concern for performance and concern for people, and may be insensitive to the fact that other people's priorities in this field may differ from their own.

Older men are more likely to make wise judgements about the implications of change, the limitations on the speed with which change can be effected and the effect on individuals. They are more likely to take a realistic view about human motivation and response to various kinds of pressures. On the other hand, they will often tend to be overcautious and follow a safe course, letting competitors monopolize revolutionary new ideas.

It is rare perhaps that a company is monopolized by a young group of managers unless it is a new company, but the other extreme is far from unusual. It is quite common to find that all the company's senior managers are approaching retirement together and often, in that situation, the company shows obvious signs of reduced vitality.

It is therefore a favourable indicator if there is an even spread of ages from the early thirties right through to the retirement age, so that both energy and experience are well represented in management discussions.

Is there a balance of personalities?

If there is a diversity of functional experience there is usually, automatically, a reasonable variety of personality types, because salesmen, accountants, engineers, personnel managers do tend to choose their careers because of their basic aptitudes which are reflected by diverse personalities. It is, however, worth considering the question. For instance, two really dominant men in one company are almost bound to clash. Another characteristic that may be relevant is the degree of optimism or pessimism present. It is pleasant to work with people who are inclined to optimism, but too much of it may lead to a disregard of proper corrective action when warning signs appear. Too much pessimism may inhibit risk-taking. As before, the essential factor is a balance between these extremes.

Are the managers trained in the basic disciplines relevant to their jobs?

Management is far from an exact science. The situation is perhaps analogous to that of engineering during the Victorian era, in that there is a great deal of empirical knowledge and some limited theoretical understanding, with many practitioners who have learnt by trial and error, rather than by systematic study. There is, however, now a substantial body of management knowledge that should be understood by every manager. There are some who ignore the rules or do not know them, and yet achieve outstanding results by intuitive judgement, but they are more likely to spend their time, if not re-inventing the wheel, at least re-inventing the steam engine.

Management education therefore is important and there are, particularly in small companies, still too many managers who have not opened a book since they left school and therefore failed to benefit by the accumulated experience of other people. A manager should have a deep knowledge of the techniques available to his own functional responsibility, and a working knowledge of those of his colleagues. A manufacturing manager, for example, should understand the basic principles of marketing and market forecasting, be familiar with the pattern of product life cycles and be conversant with the basis of pricing decisions.

Similarly, a marketing manager should be familiar with the principles of production and inventory control, value engineering, economic batch quantities and so on. In a situation in which all managers do have a deep understanding of the techniques available in their own special fields and a working knowledge of those outside their own fields, and are able to understand their colleagues' problems, they will be able to discuss with reasonable objectivity the best solutions to company-wide problems.

If this situation does not exist, there is the obvious risk that the business will not run at its best level of efficiency, and also there is likely to be a conflict between different business functions.

Other things being equal, educated and numerate managers are more likely to be successful in any given situation than those who have learnt by working with their predecessors and who work by rule-of-thumb.

Do the managers communicate effectively with each other and work together as a team?

The indications from the earlier questions may be entirely favourable and yet the managers may be working as individuals, running their own departments in the most internally effective way, but not working together as a team. Usually this depends very much on the man at the top. The chief executive must exert positive leadership. Obviously, therefore, it is important during an appraisal to form a judgement about the leadership of the chief executive, and to find out what kind of man he is and how his subordinates respond to him.

There is, however, no way of listing the characteristics that a leader will possess and, from this, being sure that a given individual will be a good leader of a management team because he possesses those characteristics. The most unexpected people prove to have the necessary characteristics for effective leadership, and others who show all the outward signs do not generate the necessary respect and loyalty. The only test of the effectiveness of the chief executive in his leadership role is the cohesiveness of the management team.

What is the current style of management?

Just as there is no one appropriate style of leader, there is no single effective management style. Some chief executives are autocrats, imposing on the company their own personality; others are essentially successful chairmen of management committees which participate deeply in decision-making.

There are as many different styles as there are individual management teams. It does not seem to be very important which style is adopted provided that all the individuals involved work well together in that situation. Obviously an individual manager who would work well under an autocratic chief executive, would be likely to find it difficult to adjust to a situation in which he was expected to make a powerful contribution to management decisions. A manager used to participative management would almost certainly be very unhappy in a more autocratic situation.

The present trend is towards a relatively free discussion within management teams, and this seems to be a favourable trend provided that, when decisions are made, they become binding on the group involved.

The particular management style is, however, important if there is any question of a merger between two companies or the acquisition of one company by another. Probably the biggest single source of difficulty in a post-merger situation is the failure of the participants to realize, in time, that their management styles are totally dissimilar. Apart from the question raised earlier—autocratic or participative management styles —there is a wide range of other characteristics that must be considered: the degree of delegation for profit responsibility, the strength of the sanctions against failure and the rewards for success, the balance between concern for people and concern for performance. These are just a few of the characteristics that differ appreciably from one company to another and which may make it difficult to merge two companies together without causing severe problems.

If a merger is under consideration, it is important not only that the management styles are compatible but that the management strengths of the two companies complement each other. It sometimes happens that companies get together because their product ranges are complementary and it is then found that their management strengths are too similar for the merger to work well. They may both, for example, have good marketing and distribution strengths and weak financial management. In such a situation the merger may well run into difficulties because of the desire of the two marketing groups to retain their independence within the enlarged company, with not enough financial muscle to force attention to the economies of joint operation.

Is there provision for succession, particularly at senior levels?

If a company is being assessed with the intention of acquisition or investment, the envisaged relationship is likely to be a reasonably permanent one. Therefore the future management situation is as relevant as the present one; there must be provision for succession. At the top level there should be at least one contender for each position, and at the lower levels a pool of good managers should ideally provide two or three managers to be seriously considered for any vacancy. The problem caused by a vacancy should be a choice between capable contenders, rather than deciding whether anyone is good enough for the job. The management scene in any company is a constantly changing one. Managers come and go, a company's needs change as it grows. A company that is growing fast can often be short of management talent just because of its growth. This is not necessarily a harmful situation provided that the quality of management is good, so that succession can be dealt with by recruitment at the lower levels and by internal promotion.

Summary

The objective of the exploration of management competence and style is to present a rounded picture of the strengths and weaknesses of the management team and if there are important weaknesses, to decide how easily they can be remedied. However, what makes a company successful is its distinctive capability. This concept predicates that profit growth is built on strengths rather that by remedying weaknesses. The study of management may therefore indicate that the chosen policies are not appropriate for the company, that other policies more closely related to the competence of the management team present a more attractive growth path. A study of management, therefore, may indicate possible weaknesses that will inhibit success and may also indicate strengths that have not been fully taken account of in formulating the company's profit plans.

Chapter Eight

MARKETING

As all income comes from the market-place, a company's marketing attitude and skills are crucial in the formulation of a profit plan and its successful implementation. In carrying out an appraisal there is a need to consider the existing markets; how well they have been researched, how fully they are understood, and to what extent products are tailored to satisfy needs identified there. It is also necessary to study the process by which a company develops its strategy. The current situation reveals how effective that process has been in the past and is a useful indicator of its effectiveness.

It is important, however, to make sure that the present situation, if satisfactory, was not due to fortuitous circumstances or as a result of a process which has already changed, perhaps adversely. It is therefore necessary to study both the current situation and the process that deals with future change. As before, exploratory discussions are based on a series of open-ended questions designed to reveal underlying attitudes. A few typical questions are indicated below.

Exploratory questions

What are the company's marketing objectives?

If the response to this question is a period of deep thought or an attempt to put together an answer on the spot, then the company does not practise the art of marketing, however good it may be at designing and selling acceptable products. A company that has not thought about and explicitly stated its marketing objectives is in a vulnerable position because it is reacting to forces without really understanding their nature and source. It may easily be moving up a blind alley into a market sector that is doomed to disappear due to underlying changes in customer needs, new technological discoveries or similar causes of changes in demand.

Any useful definition of objectives should normally be in terms of satisfying a specific range of user needs. The breadth of definition is important. If it is too wide then it does not serve much purpose as a unifying concept for the company's products. What is probably best is that there should be a broad concept defining its general objectives and then a series of objectives within specific market segments.

Such objectives would normally include statements concerning:

1 *Market posture*   This would indicate in general terms the company's planned position in the market. Does it intend to be a low cost, high volume supplier? Or to capture specialist market segments at a premium price? What will be the general extent of the range of products or services offered? What will be the general distribution pattern?

2 *Market share*   It is necessary to define the market share sought because this influences many other factors in the marketing mix and can also have an appreciable effect on product design, manufacturing facilities required, etc.

3 *Benefits offered*   The company should have a clear idea of why it expects its customers to buy from it and not from competitors. The main benefits should therefore be stated as part of the objectives.

4 *Product range*   There will be a steady process of product development and replacement so that a product range is never a fixed concept, but it would normally be possible to state as part of objectives the product plans for the next few product cycles.

The question of whether or not objectives are in existence and how they have been defined is the starting point to the exploration of the marketing strengths of the company.

Does the company have a thorough knowledge of its present markets and understand why its customers buy from it?

Market information is like military intelligence, it enables the marketing strategy to be developed on a foundation of knowledge about factors that influence a customer's buying decisions, and about what competitors are currently doing and likely to do in the future. The knowledge may be obtained by specific market surveys, by desk research, by patiently gathering individual items of information and classifying and recording them; the means of assembling the information is not important in this context. What is important is that there should be a flow of objectively grounded information which is made available in an organized way, to the company's decision-makers. If such market intelligence is not assembled on a systematic basis, then the company's marketing plans, and therefore its profit plan, must be regarded as unreliable.

What does the company consider are the factors which provide its competitive edge?

There is usually a whole range of answers to this question and they, in turn, relate back to the distinctive competence of the business. It is not possible to rank such factors in any precise order, but it is possible to regard some as being more secure than others. For example, a range of products that has been carefully designed to meet identified user needs, particularly if it has special features with patent protection, provides a relatively secure base.

A price advantage is much more easily eroded unless it is founded on manufacturing economies of a fundamental nature.

Company reputation, customer loyalty and similar characteristics, although useful in tipping the balance between closely competitive products or services, may be quite ephemeral if put to the test as customer-holding advantages.

Whatever the characteristic that provides the competitive edge, the more an intrinsic characteristic of the company it is and the more difficult it is to imitate, then the greater can be the confidence that the company's forecasts are soundly based.

What needs do the company's products or services satisfy?

This is a basic marketing question. A person usually buys a product or a service, not because he wants the product or the service, but because he has some need that can be satisfied by its use. The distinction is important because it opens up the opportunity for speculation about alternative ways of satisfying this need.

If someone buys a utilitarian product, a grinding machine for example, then it is fairly obvious that his need is to produce a surface of a certain configuration and smoothness, and that there are potentially other ways of producing a surface with similar properties. It is also obvious that if the buyer could produce the same result more cheaply without buying a grinding machine he would readily do so. In many cases a user has a number of ways of satisfying his needs, so that one group of products may be competing, not only with similar products, but with a diverse range of totally different products. Even products that have a high intrinsic value, a diamond ring for instance, are bought for similar reasons. If it is for personal adornment, or to display wealth, there are, obviously, very many other products which could satisfy the need.

Thought about the needs satisfied by the products leads directly to speculation about alternative ways of satisfying the same needs and consideration of the possibility of competitive innovation.

Could the market need be satisfied by other products currently available or potentially available as a result of foreseeable developments?

The objective of the marketing assessment is to find out whether or not the company's markets seem reasonably stable.

The purpose of looking at alternative ways of satisfying the same needs is to ensure that the study does not just concentrate on competitive products. Ocean liners on the London–New York trip even competed with each other for speed records right up to the 1950s, yet their real competitors were not other shipping companies but the aircraft flying above them. There are many companies today considering the competition only from products similar to their own, and ignoring the real competitive dangers just because they are thinking in terms of products, rather than of user needs.

It follows that well-founded sales forecasts will have considered such factors and will be based on an understanding about how user needs are likely to be satisfied in the future. The conclusions may not always be right, but they will certainly be better than could be deduced without such consideration.

If a new technology is on the horizon, when is it likely to be taking a market share, and should the company take part in its development?

It is not necessarily the best marketing strategy always to be first with a product breakthrough. A really major change is expensive and hazardous and is usually fairly slow in producing a worthwhile return.

At the present time, there is repeated discussion in the Press and elsewhere about what will replace the piston engine for powering road transport. A number of companies have spent substantial sums of money on rotary engines, both Wankel and turbine; there are also experimental steam and electric cars with quite a large number of individual design variants; another form of rotary engine has just been announced in Australia. Apart from specialist town use, the only one of these that has gained any worthwhile marketing acceptance is the Wankel engine.

The point being made here is that no manufacturer can afford to follow all development avenues, and it may be good strategy not to follow any of them until someone else has spent the large sums of money necessary to make a breakthrough, and then to buy a licence for the successful design. This is an unadventurous strategy, but for many companies a valid one.

Do customer services match those of competitors?

As has been said earlier, a customer does not buy a product, he buys satisfaction of a need. The fact that this is a cliché does not undermine its essential truth. It follows that to concentrate just on products is to miss important opportunities for maximising demand by providing additional services linked to the company's products and so improve its ability to satisfy customer needs. A company selling flooring materials, for example, may provide:

1 An advisory service to help customers choose suitable materials for a given application.
2 A complete floor laying service.
3 An after-care service.
4 A guarantee of durability and life.

If it provides these additional services, then it will be much easier for it to sell its basic products than a competitor who just concentrates on selling the products.

Often the additional service is clearly recognizable as in the above example. It is a service that requires a specific organization and resources; it may often produce its own profitable return.

There are, however, other cases where the service given is not so obviously recognizable. A company in a technical field may achieve success due to the value of the informal advice given by its sales staff to the company's customers. This service may have arisen fortuitously because of the wise choice of the field sales force, or it may have arisen as a matter of specific policy.

If the company's product appeal is being augmented in this way, then the preliminary analysis of distinctive competence should have revealed this factor. It may not, however, be easy to identify this kind of additional service provided by competitors. Taking the same illustration, it may be that one company has chosen its salesmen because of their skill at selling in the conventional sense, while another may have chosen its salesmen because of their technical knowledge. It is possible that from the same starting point the former group might produce better results in the short term, only to be overtaken by the second group in the longer term. In such circumstances a company may see its sales eroded by a competitor for reasons that are not readily recognizable.

It is important, therefore, to understand precisely what it is that competitors offer and to make an objective comparison between the company's own services and those offered by competitors. To do this properly, usually entails an independent market study, otherwise there is considerable danger of the results being prejudiced by existing attitudes.

How does a company set its prices?

If a company is producing basic materials or foodstuffs, then its prices will, almost certainly, be based on the effects of supply and demand. There will be a recognized price that no individual company can do much to modify. If such a primary producer reduces its selling prices in order to capture a bigger market share, then almost certainly its competitors will follow suit, at least in the same territories, so that the net result is that all the suppliers earn less profit. In a situation of this kind prices are generally determined by factors outside the company's control, and profitability is controlled by efficiency of production and by volume obtained through other aspects of its marketing performance.

In all other cases, which are far more numerous than the one described above, a pricing policy has a very direct bearing on profitability.

If prices are determined by adding a predetermined percentage to product cost, this is normally an indication that the full profit potential of the business is not being realized. As far as customers are concerned, the price they are willing to pay for any product or service is determined by almost anything other than what it costs to make the product or supply the service.

They are, for instance, attracted by distinctive design, special performance features, a reputation for reliability or quality, esteem value, and a whole bundle of other characteristics which decide how well the product satisfies their needs or desires.

Before making such a decision to buy (in which there are many subconscious factors) they will also take into account what competitors offer them. The price that can be charged for a product or a service will therefore depend on how well it fills a customer's need compared with the cost to him of alternative ways of filling the same need. This is the only important pricing consideration.

A product with distinctive features may therefore command a very high margin over its cost, whereas a 'standard' product competing with a range of products not markedly dissimilar, will command a much lower margin.

A cost-plus pricing system will generally fail to obtain the high margins for the 'special' products. It may also fail in the other direction in that it may price 'standard' products at too high a level and so lose turnover, when they could have been sold at an appropriate market price and still made a satisfactory contribution to profit.

It follows that the only really satisfactory pricing method is a detailed comparison between a company's own products and those of its competitors, and an attempt to analyse the different features in terms of benefits to the purchaser. This is, of course, an imperfect process. There is no arithmetical way of arriving at the correct answer, but nevertheless the attempt must be made because there is no satisfactory alternative.

Some companies claim to price according to the market situation, when they are really following a price leader. In some circumstances this is a necessary process. A small supplier producing a standard product in a market dominated by much larger companies may well decide that this is the only way it can set its prices. On the whole, though, a company in that situation does not seem likely to be a very good investment unless there are other special reasons for its survival.

If a company is pricing on a cost-plus basis, there is almost always scope for profit improvement and, therefore, the company's own profit forecast may be too conservative. On the other hand the use of this technique indicates a lack of understanding of market forces and therefore perhaps a weakness in sales forecasting in general.

How was the market forecast developed?

This is a very important question because the sales forecast is a foundation for all the company's budgets. In some companies the sales forecast is produced just by adding a percentage to the previous year's actual sales turnover, and then trying to justify it by assumptions about the market. Worse still, is the practice, by no means unusual, of starting with the profit expectations, calculating the turnover necessary to produce the indicated profit, and then treating that as a sales forecast. Such methods are, of course, quite unsatisfactory as a means of determining company budgets and even worse when they are used to assess profit potential.

The only satisfactory way of preparing a sales forecast is to gather sufficient market intelligence to understand what forces are operating in the market and to judge their likely effect in the next few years, and then to assess the effect of company initiatives designed to maintain or improve its position in specific parts of the market.

In other words, changes in turnover will arise because of external circumstances, internal decisions and initiatives, and luck. A serious study of the first two of these influences is better than depending too much on the third one.

The quality of a market forecast depends, therefore, on the amount of information the company has and the amount of detailed consideration it has given to the forecasting problem. Compared with these two factors the particular techniques of forecasting are less important.

What control data are available to the top marketing executive?

To manage effectively, an executive needs to know for each sales period, at the very minimum:

1 Sales by territory.
2 Sales by product group.
3 Profit contribution from each product group.
4 Selling costs broken down by categories.

These are very basic requirements. In most companies other items of information would also be important. To be really useful the information should be presented together with budget or forecast figures.

During an appraisal such information is very necessary in order to confirm whether or not the current trends are satisfactory. Apart from that, if data are inadequate this is normally a reflection on the adequacy of the management team.

In a very small company the absence of routine control data may be slightly less important than suggested above because the executives concerned will have a direct knowledge of the day-to-day situation, but a company very rapidly outgrows such a situation.

Are distribution methods suitable or will they require development if the general market plan is to be achieved?

Most distribution systems just grow. When a company is small and struggling to survive, it tends to sell to whoever will pay enough money for the products or services it offers, and is not much worried about the interaction between individual customers. With growth, there comes a need to decide more formally such matters as pricing and discount policies and levels of service to particular types of customer, if only to ensure that the most profitable product mix is sold. At some time, the question of some form of vertical intergration may have to be considered. A manufacturer has to decide whether or not to buy wholesale or retail companies and so get some control over distribution channels. Even if this is not part of an offensive strategy, it may well be necessary as a defensive step to stop too much of a distribution network falling into the hands of a major competitor.

Companies are becoming increasingly aware of the importance of the marketing function and, therefore, of being in direct touch with their eventual customers. This is possible only if each link in the distribution chain is under their own control. This awareness has brought with it a much greater interest in building distribution strength.

If the company already controls its own distribution facilities then its turnover is not subject to fluctuations caused by decisions by intermediate distributors. This is a source of strength that adds credibility to the sales forecast.

If the company sells all its products through intermediate distributors, then there is a need to examine the security of distribution. How easily, for example, could the distributors turn to another supplier for a similar range of products? If they did so, how else would the company market its products and what would be the effect of the period of disruption? It may be that the company has invested heavily in direct advertising and thus generated high distribution strength through customer demand. This may be effective provided that the product is distinctive. On the other hand, if it is easy for the salesman to substitute another product at the final selling stage, the company may still be vulnerable to adverse decisions by distributors despite the market suction which it has generated. An assessment of the degree of vulnerability to such action is therefore necessary.

Summary

A company that has an informed understanding of its market will usually be able to prepare sound market forecasts, make the right marketing decisions, and therefore achieve satisfactory growth. A company that lacks such market understanding will not necessarily be unsuccessful in the short term, but its performance is likely to be more erratic and it will probably suffer profit reverses at times of accelerated market change.

Chapter Nine

NEW PRODUCT DEVELOPMENT

A company's marketing plans will almost certainly show a gap between the desired turnover and that which can be expected from products and services currently offered to the market. The normal expectation is that this gap will be filled by developing and marketing new products. The reason that such a gap exists is that, as is well-known, all products and all services have a limited life cycle. At any given time some of the company's products or services will have entered a period of declining market demand. Because of lower volume and competition from more recently designed products, they will also be providing a reduced profit contribution.

In an effectively managed company there will be sufficient products under development, not only to replace those which are declining, but in addition to provide growth. The proportion of a company's resources that has to be devoted to this varies considerably from one company to another. It is, for example, obviously much higher in a couture house producing high-fashion clothes where the whole product range is obsolete after one season, than it is in a business producing men's shoes, where although there is a need for product renewal, a particular design can be expected to be in the company's range for a number of years.

There are some fields in which the rate of product renewal

can be relatively low. Many hand tools, for example, are similar in basic form to those used by several generations past but, even there, differences in the steels used, new handle shapes for comfort and ease of working, new handle materials for durability, all cause an established range of products to become unattractive in the market-place and so to be redesigned.

A process of product renewal is, therefore, an essential feature of any company. The effectiveness with which it is organized is an important determinant of profit potential. If a company does not have an organised system of product renewal, and a supply of new products in the pipeline, that in itself may be an indication that there is something seriously wrong with the management of the company. It is also a warning to examine very carefully the assumptions on which the sales forecast has been prepared.

It may be that a study shows that there are too few new products under development, even though the short-term sales position still looks relatively satisfactory. In this case there is a need to estimate how long it will take to develop new products right through the cycle including:

1 Identification of market needs.
2 Definition of product range.
3 Design study.
4 Manufacture of samples or prototypes.
5 Testing and modification of prototypes.
6 Ordering of tools, jigs, etc.
7 Obtaining plant.
8 Ordering materials and components.
9 Manufacture of first production run.
10 Establishment of the product in its market growth phase.

This time scale can be considerably longer than first estimates would indicate. There may perhaps be a danger that, because of unforeseen causes of delay, development may take place under considerable time pressure so that the products, when developed, are not as satisfactory as they should have been, with resultant harm to the quality image that the company is perhaps seeking to develop or maintain.

In making these comments it is not intended to take too pessimistic a view. A company at a relatively low ebb because of lack of management drive can often be a very attractive opportunity for the injection of new management and capital, provided that it has sufficient strengths to form a foundation for growth. It is however necessary to beware of underestimating the product renewal time.

It is essential, therefore, to investigate a company's capability of providing such new products at the required rate and with the necessary perception about market requirements.

Exploratory questions

As before, there is a need to explore certain general questions in order to build up a picture of the company's situation.

Where are the present products on their life cycle curves?

As mentioned earlier, every product has a limited life cycle. The general shape of the life cycle curve is shown in Figure 9.1. This shows six different phases through which any product (or service) can be considered to pass. There are other valid ways of subdividing the curve, but this does not affect the general principles involved. The lower line on the same graph represents the pattern of cash flows for a typical project.

During the product development phase there are only negative cash flows as money is invested in design costs and the production of prototypes. Then follows the product launch and the market development phase during which test marketing takes place. During this phase, although products are being sold on the market, they are usually being sold at a loss and cash flows are still negative.

As the product gains greater market acceptance, a rapid growth phase follows; during this period unit production costs fall as a direct result of increased volume of output and the effect of the learning process on the productivity of all employees. During this time the product starts to generate profits and, therefore, the direction of cash flow will be reversed. The maturity phase follows, during which sales grow at a reduced rate. Profits are still very satisfactory, but towards the end of the maturity phase competitive products exert pressures that inhibit further growth.

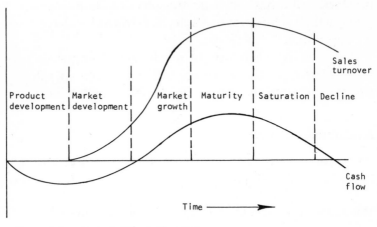

Figure 9.1   Product life cycle curve

During the next phase, saturation is reached. There are more products available than the market can absorb, competition becomes more intensive and prices fall. At some stage, a competitor brings out a new product range which is designed to satisfy the same market need, in a more effective way; the existing product range then enters a period of decline. It may continue to produce profits for an appreciable period, but eventually will cease to make a positive contribution.

This is a typical picture. Of course, in real life the curve is distorted by a great range of factors, for example:

1 New uses may be discovered for old products.
2 A new group of users may emerge due to such factors as shifts in social attitudes or fashion, or by geographical market extension.
3 Legislation may be introduced which enforces product change, for example, to eliminate pollution or improve safety.
4 Changes in parity of money may render foreign products suddenly more or less competitive.

There is an endless list of possibilities. The point being made here is that the curve is only a very general representation. Its length too can vary between very wide extremes and there are no rules that can define this, only experience in a particular market with a particular kind of product.

As well as the individual product life cycle, a product category as a whole has its own life cycle which is an envelope of the life cycles of the individual products in the category. For example, the product category of 35-mm rangefinder cameras started in the 1930s, reached its peak in the 1950s, and is now experiencing a decline under the competitive onslaught of a new category of single-lens reflex cameras. Within that time span many individual products went through their individual life cycles and made their contribution to the product category.

One illustration of how patterns of product category life cycles can change in perhaps unexpected ways is given by the current demand for motorcycles by young Americans in relatively high income groups. Until the 1960s, motorcycles tended to be the mode of transport used by people who could not afford cars. Even when they were used for sport it was mainly by people who, if they had had more money, would have preferred sports cars. Against this pattern it seemed inevitable that, as individual communities became more affluent, the sales of motorcycles would decline and, indeed, this was the pattern which seemed to be emerging. Then the pattern seems to have changed. It has become fashionable in certain circles, particularly in the United States, for relatively wealthy young men to buy motorcycles for pleasure use; so that a motorcycle instead of being a poor man's mode of transport has become an affluent man's means of self-expression. Whatever the reason, the demand pattern, and therefore the product category life cycle, has been changed in a significant way.

There is a need to know, therefore, the state of the company's products in relation to their individual life cycles, and also what is happening to the life cycle of the particular product category. The obvious indicators apply, namely:

1 Past and current growth patterns.

  2 Past and current profitability levels.
  3 Comparison with competitive products.
  4 Identified opportunities for further market development.
  5 Ideas for alternative uses for the product.

The position of a company's products on their life cycle curves obviously has a serious effect on the forecasts of future profitability. If a substantial proportion of the products are in the later stages, then there is a clear need for investment in new product development, and some decline in sales must be expected while new products are developed and brought into the market. In such circumstances a very profitable company may be a bad investment.

If the reverse situation applies, and the majority of products are in the early part of their product life cycles, then current profitability is likely to be low, but with a good opportunity for a substantial profit improvement without much immediate investment. The only real danger in this situation is that some products will fail in their development stages and never realize their implied potential.

Ideally, but rarely in real life, there will be a balanced range of products at all stages of development, and when this is found in a company it is a healthy sign for its future.

How suitable are the company's present products to the market needs they are satisfying?

The study of marketing will have provided an answer to this question from the point of view of the company's customers, which is obviously of great importance. Nevertheless, within the product design department there may be a different viewpoint and additional information which is also valuable in arriving at a sound judgement about the product range. The company's designers may know, for example, that a new process just introduced, perhaps in another country, may represent a serious competitive threat not yet apparent to the market in general. Customers may be quite satisfied with what they have because they have not yet had the alternative presented to them. The replacement of strut jib cranes by telescopic jib cranes was one example of the collapse of the life cycle of one product category, which was not anticipated by the market and therefore not revealed by a market study; yet engineers in the industry were well aware that such a change was on its way.

How profitable are individual parts of the product range?

It is rarely true that individual parts of a product range are equally profitable. One aspect of successful marketing strategy is to make sure that each product that has a distinctive performance, appearance, market image, or other market advantage, is given a premium price. In a well-run company pricing will be a major management pre-occupation and the margins for each group of products will be carefully adjusted to maximize profitability.

It is therefore to be expected that there are differences in profitability between different parts of the product range. Provided such differences are known, and have been introduced as part of the marketing plan, this is an indication of management competence.

If, however, the differences in profit margin arise only from an accidental combination of circumstances, they may not even be known to exist. It is far from uncommon to find companies in which part of the product range is losing money, either because the company does not realize that losses are being incurred, or because managers believe it to be necessary to include certain loss-making products in their range to provide a comprehensive range to their customers.

The latter assumption may be valid in certain situations, but in most cases it will be untrue. The problem is usually one of inertia. It is easy to say that customers will object if the product is withdrawn, and difficult to prove the reverse without actually withdrawing it.

During an appraisal of profit potential it is necessary to know what would be the effect on the short-term profitability of ceasing to manufacture such loss-making products. This leads to a straightforward choice between accepting the current situation, increasing certain prices in order to enhance profitability, or ceasing to supply.

If the profitability of individual products or product groups is not known with reasonable precision, that in itself is an indication that something is wrong with the company's financial information systems. It also means that decisions about product mix, marketing policies, pricing decisions, cannot have been made on a valid basis.

Is the product range broad enough to survive unforeseen competitive innovation?

One-product companies are notoriously vulnerable to shifts in market demand. On the other hand, if the one product (or, more likely, a narrow range of products) has been well designed, and the company has been able to use all its resources to develop one particular market segment, then the profitability from so doing may be very high. For this reason, it is often a good strategy to attack a market on a narrow front and to achieve penetration in depth in a specific field. However, persistence in this approach, after the initial market development, creates the risk of a serious setback (unless there is a virtual certainty that the demand for the product will continue, and the company is relatively invulnerable to competition; which is a rare situation.)

It is very difficult to generalize about what is required to provide relative security from really determined and aggressive competition. The alternative to narrow specialization is certainly not to scatter products over a very wide range, but to try to secure market penetration in depth in a selected number of market sectors. For example, a company in the electronics industry may well be in the mass production of radio and TV sets, in commercial communication equipment, and in the military electronics industry. These three markets are affected by quite different market forces and it would, therefore, be an unlikely coincidence if all were affected at the same time by market conditions or competitive action. If the same company were making radio and TV sets, refrigerators, and electric fires and cookers, which are all consumer products, it is likely that the market would be affected by similar forces at the same time and, therefore, from a defensive point of view the range of products is far less satisfactory.

Is there excessive product variety?

This is the obverse of the previous question. As has been said earlier, products enter a phase of decline, but there is rarely a sharp cut-off. Some sales will be obtained almost indefinitely. If there is not determined management action, products may remain in the company's range long after they have ceased to make a worthwhile contribution to profitability. The effect is sometimes masked because if one compares direct cost (including an average allocation of overheads) with the selling price, the product may still appear to be profitable. What is overlooked is that the clutter in the product range causes excess costs at almost every overhead level, obscures the company's market image, overloads the sales force, and leaves customers with a feeling that the company is old-fashioned, to be used only for the obsolete, expensive spare parts, etc. Meanwhile, the cost of maintaining a big inventory has also pushed up the overhead costs allocated to the higher volume products.

An excessive product range is a common contributor to company decline. Each product should form part of a comprehensive, planned pattern; any product that does not fit the pattern should be eliminated from the range. Excessive product variety spells danger to profits and is a symptom of decline.

In searching for new product ideas, does the company look inwards at its own manufacturing and design skills, or outwards to the needs of its customers?

To be successful every company needs to build on its own distinctive competence. If the distinctive competence includes special manufacturing strengths or design skills, then it is natural that new products should be specified to take maximum advantage of these. There is a danger, however, that a company may extend this too far and take an inadequate account of market needs. It will develop products to satisfy needs that it believes the market should have, rather than those that the market actually does have. The inward-looking company can be very successful if its own design staff have flair and a good intuitive feeling for the market, but can be very vulnerable to market changes. In such companies there is a risk that the views of the design staff become self-reinforcing and if a product does not sell 'as it should', more energy is devoted to showing how foolish the customer is in not buying the product, than is devoted to finding out what the customer really wants and designing that.

A company that looks outwards at the needs of its customers before specifying new products is in a much stronger position. It may at times be wrong in its decisions, but the probability of products being developed which fail to appeal to the market is very much lower than would be likely in the case of the inward-looking company.

Is the selection of new products made by a systematic evaluation?

Even if the company is looking outwards at the market to develop new product ideas, there is still a need to establish an organized system to evaluate new product ideas. Normally this consists of a process of narrowing down the company's marketing objectives until the needs for a specific product range emerges as a natural outcome of the process. First the general market concepts are defined, then particular segments are selected for development, then particular customer needs within those segments are identified, which enables product ranges to be specified to meet those needs. This is the typical orderly process and, in the normal course of business, is the most likely source of growth and profitability.

The creative element can support or disrupt this process. A supportive approach would be to think very deeply about market needs and then develop products satisfying those needs in a uniquely effective way. The alternative, which is to throw up a disparate stream of new product ideas, may provide such a brilliant breakthrough that it allows the company to outperform all its competitors. This kind of breakthrough captures the imagination and has led to some great successes, but is far less reliable as a process than the systematic step-by-step approach.

The presence of systematic approach to the selection of new products, based on market need, indicates that development effort is probably being expended in a useful way and is therefore a favourable indicator. If the selection of new products is on an opportunistic basis, there must be doubts about the utilization of development resources and some reservation about growth forecasts.

Are there clear decision points during new product development, or does each product grow in an uncontrolled fashion?

In the course of developing a new product, there are normally stages, which are relatively easy to define in the given business context, at which the development process can be monitored to make sure that the product or process being developed meets the planned specification, both in terms of performance and cost. Such systematic monitoring can prevent new products under development drifting away from the original design intentions and becoming too expensive or too complex, or failing to meet essential performance requirements. Such a monitoring system also enables development performance to be controlled against programme requirements so that, if development shows signs of lagging behind programme, remedial action can take place.

How are new products developed, how many minds trained in different disciplines contribute?

A narrow base for product development is a source of risk. To have a diversity of contribution from within the company at the time new product ideas are being reviewed and when development is in process, is usually a source of strength. As indicated, a marketing viewpoint is essential; but if, right at the beginning, the views of the production management team, the production engineers, the cost accountants, the buying department and the quality control department are sought as well as those of the product design section and drawing office, a product idea is more likely to start its life with requirements for low cost, ease of manufacture, reliability and durability, built in at the design stage. It is much easier to do this than for the design department to develop it in isolation and then attempt to reduce the product's prime cost, or improve its reliability, at some later stage.

Is quality and reliability systematically engineered into products and processes?

Quality starts in the design department. Any product has certain intrinsic performance characteristics. Its durability is largely controlled by such matters as the materials used, the way in which disparate materials are joined together by stitching, riveting, welding, glueing, bonding, etc., and by the designer's judgement about the kinds of extreme conditions in which the product will be used. From a design point of view this is usually a matter of making sure that the design is a balanced one, with each of the components making an even contribution to product life, and with no weak links in the chain.

It is obvious that if a product is designed so that one component is inadequate, then there will be early failures and customer dissatisfaction so that the company's products as a whole will fall into disrepute. It is perhaps not quite so obvious that if the reverse happens, that one or more components are much stronger or more durable than they need be, this may in certain circumstances be equally harmful. An example which comes to mind is in the motor industry where, in the past it was thought that a very strong chassis frame would give protection in an accident, but where it is now realized that it is necessary to make sure that the vehicle ends will crumble, leaving only the central cage intact.

The more common effect of making a number of components in a complete product more durable than necessary is that additional costs are incurred without providing the customer with any additional value. It is important, therefore, that quality is engineered from the start as a conscious part of the design process.

Another aspect of ensuring durability is designing so that manufacturing faults are unlikely. There can be two products which, if manufactured to specification, will perform equally well and be equally durable. However, if in one case it is more difficult to make the product to the specified standard, then on average this product will fail more often in service. The difficulty may be a requirement for more precise standards, closer tolerances of machining for example, or it may be a matter of more complex assembly and therefore a higher probability of mistakes.

Designing for quality and reliability is therefore a matter of engineering into the product balanced durability and ease of manufacture. This can only be done at the design stage.

There is nothing about a company's marketing reputation that lingers in the public mind as long as weakness in quality. It is very easy to get a bad reputation and it can take a lifetime to recover the situation.

If the company is being considered for acquisition, it is very important to know as much as possible about its product quality. It is usually unwise to base much value on the company's own assessment of this, because it is rare for a company not to claim that product quality is one of its competitive advantages. It is therefore necessary to make inquiries in the market-place to find out what the reputation of the company really is like.

Are the products engineered to defined cost/value standards?

Products have a tendency to escalate in cost during the development stages, sometimes owing to lack of attention to value engineering, and at other times owing to the steady accretion of additional facilities which were not included in the original specification. It sometimes happens that, in this way, a product is developed that is technically very interesting, but more elaborate than the customer really requires, and therefore too expensive to achieve its planned market share.

Successful companies critically monitor cost at all stages of development to ensure that the eventual product cost is in line with the original specification. Similarly, product performance features are monitored to ensure that additional features are incorporated only if they offer a worthwhile benefit to the customer which is not outweighed by additional cost.

Are licensing opportunities realistically explored?

A business completely dependent on manufacturing and selling other people's products under licence tends to be vulnerable unless there is appreciable product diversity, because it lacks the ability to control its own future in at least one important sense—product innovation. On the other hand, a company that draws a proportion of its products by marketing (and possibly manufacturing) products under licence which have been designed elsewhere, perhaps abroad, may gain some healthy contributions to its profits.

Similarly, a company can make additional profits by having its own designs manufactured and sold under licence in territories in which it does not itself directly market.

In considering profit potential the active consideration of licensing arrangements in both directions is an indicator of strength; overdependence on manufacturing other people's products under licence is a sign of relative weakness.

Are adequate resources allocated for new product development purposes?

Assuming that there are no dramatic changes in a company's circumstances in terms of the markets it is serving and the product ranges being developed for those markets; then, on average, a given expenditure on product development will produce a predictable future turnover from the sales of the newly developed products. (This is true only by taking an average over a reasonable large number of new products; the turnover derived from individual developments will, of course, not bear a very close relationship with the development cost.)

If it is intended to increase turnover, it is generally necessary, therefore, to increase the expenditure on new product development approximately in proportion to the increased turnover required, and well before the required date.

The ratio between development cost and turnover obviously

varies appreciably from one company to another, as does the time delay between the development expenditure and its effect on turnover. These must be determined for the company concerned. It is therefore necessary to examine in some detail the extent of the company's resources for new product development, to decide whether they are adequate to support the planned turnover.

The time required to increase such resources can be considerable. For example, if it is decided to recruit new designers, the selection process itself may take several months and, even when the new members join the company's design team, they will take some time to get sufficiently immersed in the company's general culture to make a useful contribution. It is therefore necessary to beware of a product replenishment programme that calls for larger design resources than the company has available.

If there is a shortage of resources for new product development it is sometimes possible by uprating existing products or by improving their visual design to make a specially economical use of development resources, and it may be necessary to do this while permanent staff, etc., and additional facilities are being provided.

Summary

A company with an organized process for new product development, based on careful market study, and systematic control of all stages of development from product selection right through to the monitoring of production, is likely to consistently produce above average profits. If there is lack of systematic organization in the field of new product development, then special design flair may bridge the gap temporarily but long-term performance is unlikely to be satisfactory.

The proportion of its resources that a company needs to devote to such an activity varies from one industry to another, but for a particular company can usually be deduced by an analysis of past performance. As there is considerable lag between the application of additional development resources and the profit outcome, any decision to increase the rate of product development may well lead to a short-term fall in profit, even though it may be necessary for long-term performance.

Chapter Ten

MANUFACTURING

The effectiveness of manufacturing is relatively easy to assess because it is one of the more tangible aspects of company performance.

It is common to find that, in the manufacture of a given type of product, a number of companies have reached a roughly equivalent level of efficiency which is difficult to break through, and a number of other companies have lagged behind and are less effective to a varying degree. The primary question to be decided, therefore, is whether the company in question is approaching a 'standard' efficiency level or whether appreciable improvements are possible. Of course this standard is never constant; as new materials and manufacturing techniques become available, the acceptable standard of manufacturing effectiveness will increase. The better companies in industry keep abreast of such changes and, therefore, their standards of performance are likely to move forward in step. If a company is well below the optimum level in efficiency, it is necessary to estimate the potential benefit in reaching that level, and the cost of providing the additional plant or other facilities required to achieve it.

Manufacturing costs are also affected by product design. Good design can minimize product costs, particularly in the use of materials and in the costs of manufacturing processes. It can also lead to products that are relatively free from quality problems. Design and manufacturing are, of course, closely interlinked and there is considerable feedback between them; the existence of efficient manufacturing resources will influence the design approach which in turn will give rise to the need to develop new manufacturing skills.

An important factor in determining both the design approach and manufacturing methods is the volume of demand expected to be generated for a product. A design which may be cost effective for high volume production, may be quite inappropriate for small batch manufacture, and vice versa. Manufacturing efficiency, therefore, cannot be considered in isolation, but only in relation to design standards and potential sales volume.

As a general rule, while a company's manufacturing performance may be below the optimum level, it is not easy for it to exceed that level to a substantial degree. It is therefore unusual for a company's distinctive competence to lie, to an appreciable extent, in its manufacturing strengths.

An exception to this could be a company possessing unusual craft skills. Two cases which come to mind are the hand decoration of high grade pottery and the manufacture of hand-made furniture, both of which require high skill levels, which may provide an important competitive advantage. If such skills are claimed to exist there should be a very careful examination of the market and of alternative manufacturing processes, to make quite sure that such levels of skill are required to satisfy the needs of the users of the company's products. It is sometimes found that traditional craft methods are being used although no loss of product quality would be caused by mechanization of some of the operations.

In the works of at least one famous gunmaker, for example, even taps and dies to produce screw threads were made by hand. These obviously cost a great deal more than machine-made ones, and the threads produced were less precise and less uniform. When guns were received for repair, matching parts had to be specially produced. This expensive and laborious process in no way improved product quality. On the other hand, the individual filing and polishing of parts during the fitting process were important and did make a great deal of difference to quality. In situations like this, it is necessary to be discerning about those craft skills which really make a difference to the product and those which have been retained purely for traditional reasons.

Exploratory questions

In this case the exploratory questions are designed primarily to decide whether the company's manufacturing facilities are likely to be at least as effective as its competitors.

How does the company's productivity compare with the attainable standard using present methods?

It is not too difficult to assess the efficiency of a factory with reasonable accuracy. Even on a first walk round, the proportion of employees actually working, compared with those who are at the time unoccupied, will give a first indication of productivity. A more serious way of achieving the same object is to carry out a process of activity sampling (which is an attempt to make much the same assessment on a sufficient number of occasions to provide a statistically valid result). This technique needs care in certain highly specialized manufacturing situations. If rate of output is controlled by a machine process, for example, a machine minder may appear to be idle even when his machine is performing at a very satisfactory rate; if output is process controlled it is the process that should be subjected to the activity sampling, rather than the operative.

It is generally safe to assume that if the efficiency of a given plant has not been the subject of systematic study by industrial engineers, productivity can be improved by at least a third. A similar potential improvement exists if labour controlled processes are being carried out under time-work conditions.

These two potential improvements must not, however, be added together because they overlap considerably; but if, for labour-controlled processes, there has been no systematic production engineering and there is no incentive scheme, a 50 per cent improvement in productivity could reasonably be achieved.

This does not apply if output is largely controlled by machine processes. In this case the potential improvement can be assessed only by comparing the actual machine running time with that theoretically achievable (after making an appropriate allowance for time spent in changing from one product to another and for breakdowns, maintenance periods, etc.). It therefore requires a study of each of the key processes.

The answer to this question, therefore, indicates the degree to which it is possible to improve performance without major investment; it makes it possible to calculate the potential effect of this on profitability. The latter calculation depends also on the extent to which the potential improvement in profitability can be used to support additional sales, or how far it will merely result in a reduction in the direct labour hours required.

Obviously, an appreciable time is required to generate any improvement, and this must be evaluated for the specific situation, taking account of the nature of the changes envisaged.

How far can productivity be improved by a combination of new methods and plant?

This is more difficult to answer as to do so requires considerable knowledge of the manufacturing processes involved. One way of reaching a quick estimate is to consider selected key processes, estimate how far they could be improved by new plant, and then make the assumption that similar ratios apply to other processes.

Another way of approaching the problem is to examine the age spectrum of existing plant and then, by discussion with experts in the appropriate fields, to form a judgement about how far the average productivity of such plant items has improved during the period in question. It is generally fair to estimate that if a particular machine tool is kept in use more than—say—ten years, it is considerably less productive than the equivalent current design. A company that replaces over a seven to ten year depreciation cycle, and therefore has plant which on average is four to five years old, should be in a reasonably healthy condition. If the average age of plant goes much beyond five years, the company could be suffering from low levels of productivity as a consequence.

This is true only when considerating general manufacturing. In the case of major process plant, some individual items may be expected to be used for twenty to thirty years or more before replacement. The matter needs to be examined in the light of the particular industry and the company's own processes and circumstances.

If the existing plant is out of date to the extent that productivity can be appreciably improved by its replacement, then it is necessary to estimate the cost of replacement and the probable return on such an investment. (The use of discounted cash flow methods of analysis are indicated in this situation.)

Is sufficient management effort employed in the critical examination of current practices?

The answer to this question can throw a great deal of light on the two previous ones. In an efficient company a production engineering department (or in a small company a single engineer) will have specific responsibility for developing improvements in methods of manufacture. By contrast, where this is not the case production methods will typically be left for the line supervisors who will devote to the improvement of methods the small amount of time they have available from their other responsibilities. Being busy men, they will usually continue to go on using existing methods.

Another field in which continuous review is important is in the field of value engineering. As was indicated earlier, the most fruitful source of reduction in manufacturing cost is product redesign. The best way of achieving this is to have a continuous programme of value engineering so that all new products are designed from the start with proper consideration of the cost/value relationship, and existing products are re-examined at predetermined intervals to take account of new materials and processes. The existence of a specialist department engaged in the review of production methods, and the use of value engineering techniques are, therefore, indicators of potential competitive strength.

When this question and the two previous ones have been answered, it becomes possible to make an assessment of the degree to which productivity can be improved, and the cost of achieving such an improvement.

How quickly could the works deliver new product lines?

It was earlier suggested that the time scale for the introduction of new products is often underestimated. Inherent in any profit plan is an assumption about the number of new products that will be brought to the market. To test whether this is feasible, the speed with which they can be introduced into production will have to be investigated. This can usually be done best by looking at records of past achievement in this field; the presence or absence of a process of monitoring, as discussed in the previous chapter, is also a useful indicator of likely performance.

Is production control effective and are stocks and work-in-progress held within agreed standards?

In some companies production is under effective control; products are made more or less according to a defined programme which is subject to regular review as the market demand changes; any departures from programme are quickly corrected. In other companies appreciable departures from an agreed programme are the norm; the delivery date of a product depends less on a plan and more on the energetic activities of a group of progress chasers. In the latter case progress chasers may be competing with one another for the use of the same resources to obtain output of the product ranges for which they are responsible.

Obviously if a profit plan is to be achieved, it is essential that the production targets are met. The effectiveness of production control is therefore one useful indicator of the reliability of the profit forecast.

Production control is inextricably linked with the control of levels of stock and work-in-progress. If the production plan is not substantially achieved, stocks and work-in-progress will not be maintained within planned levels. Every job whose start is delayed adds to the stock of raw materials and purchased components; every job held up on the shopfloor adds to the level of work-in-progress. There is a need, therefore, to examine stock control systems and the way they are used in practice.

The ratio between stocks of material and work-in-progress and annual material usage is an important index. Comparisons can be made with the company's own performance in past periods, the performance of other companies producing similar products, or with the figures for the industry as a whole. It is unwise, however, to rely too much on the latter comparison because some very different companies can come under the same industrial classification, although they have widely different inherent stock/material usage ratios. Once the current ratio is established and a view has been taken about the attainable ratio, it is possible to assess the level of stocks and work-in-progress necessary to sustain any given turnover level. This in turn makes it possible to form an assessment of the additional working capital required to support growth in turnover, or the savings which could arise from a better stock control system.

How do delivery dates compare with those of competitors and with promises given to customers?

Nothing more separates companies that are well managed and potentially highly profitable from those that are just surviving than their attitude towards meeting their obligations to their customers. It is worth taking, therefore, a random sample of orders received by the business and comparing the promises given to customers with the actual delivery dates. Obviously this comparison will not show a satisfactory result unless production control is effective; but it is possible to have a satisfactory production control system without necessarily meeting promises given to customers. For example, promises may be given by the sales department without reference to the factory. This is sometimes done just as a means of getting orders even when it is known that the specified delivery dates will probably not be met.

In some companies the delivery period is on average as promised, but the spread of deliveries about this average is such that about half the orders are delivered late. Most industrial customers will be almost as critical of early as of late delivery because early delivery, if accepted, will unnecessarily tie up their funds. What is required, therefore, is that on average delivery should be within the period specified and that the scatter around the average should be small.

It is also important that delivery dates should compare favourably with those offered by competitors. It is worth checking, therefore, with the market appraisal in order to establish this piece of information. If competitors can consistently deliver in a shorter time, an inference can be made about their manufacturing methods or their methods of controlling and manufacturing for stock.

If a company consistently fails to deliver on time, this throws considerable doubt on the value of the production forecasts included in the profit plan. It also makes it vulnerable to new competition. Worst of all, it indicates serious failure to manage effectively.

How effectively are the available sites and buildings employed?

The examples of entrepreneurs buying existing companies at a relatively low state of profitability, selling off some of the factories and making substantially more profit than ever before, are too common to need detailing here. A critical study of the utilization of sites and buildings is, therefore, an essential part of the evaluation of profit potential; the existence of spare resources, particularly in this context, can make an otherwise unattractive investment of great interest.

Is the factory layout satisfactory, or should it be improved?

If there is effective production engineering within the company, then it will probably be found that the production flow is in one general direction with relatively small movements between operations. On the other hand, particularly if systematic production engineering is not standard practice, it may be found that individual products travel considerable distances through the plant, with much backtracking, and as a consequence many unnecessary material floats to take account of the handling delays.

It is worth examining, therefore, the paths of a random sample of products through the factory. If a logical and orderly pattern does not emerge then, almost certainly, overhead costs are higher than they need be due to excessive material handling costs, and also a considerable amount of floor space is being wasted. Better plant layout could therefore make the space available to increase production, or for disposal.

Is the plant and machinery in good condition and is it renewed on an economic replacement plan?

A visual inspection will show whether plant and machinery is in good condition; an examination of plant records will give its age and indicate the company's replacement policy. It is still worth finding out whether or not this is systematically planned or done on an *ad hoc* basis. If there is a systematic plan then the basis of the plan merits examination.

There are many companies that buy new, expensive items of plant in order to follow a breakthrough in technology without really considering how relevant this is to their own particular needs. A great deal of modern plant therefore does not necessarily mean that the equipment is contributing to better than average manufacturing performance.

This can be illustrated by the first surge of computer installations. Many companies bought a computer because it was fashionable to have one, rather than because they had found a sound economic reason for the purchase. Many of the early applications had to be withdrawn and, of course, computer installations now tend to be regarded with a good deal of scepticism; but a similar attitude existed, to a lesser degree, when numerically controlled machines became available. Many companies bought machines which were unsuitable for their particular purposes in the first rush of enthusiasm for the technique.

Of course, these are relatively exceptional circumstances. There is little doubt that a factory equipped with up-to-date machinery is normally more soundly based than one where the machinery is generally rather old.

A much more common situation is that machines are retained long after they have ceased to be adequately productive, on the ground—say—that they are only used for two days a week on a specific product and therefore it is not worth replacing them. This is often a spurious argument because in most cases there is a better way of making the same component without an underloaded special-purpose machine. It may be better, for instance, to subcontract that particular operation and make the floor space available for more productive use.

The object of an examination of a plant replacement policy is, therefore, to make sure that the plant is relatively up-to-date and suitable for its purpose, and that there are no white elephants.

Are adequate quality standards maintained?

It was said in Chapter Nine that quality and reliability must be engineered into a product in the design department. Nevertheless, it is necessary to make sure that the designer's intentions are carried out in the manufacturing processes and that quality is maintained at each manufacturing stage.

There are almost always a number of ways of producing a given product, or of carrying out a given assembly. Some of those ways are more likely to produce errors than others. For example, in an engineering factory, careful jig design can often make sure that a product cannot be misassembled. A well laid out work area, good lighting and planned training, are all factors which tend to support high quality standards.

Many companies, if asked about their quality standards, will point out that they have a large and well-organized inspection department, that each product is inspected at many stages during manufacture and, therefore, that there is a high standard of quality control. This may easily be a fallacy; an inspection department is necessary to monitor standards, but unless quality is built in, it cannot be inspected in.

If many manufacturing faults are found in a product, there is a tendency in some companies to add more and more inspection stages in an attempt to put the matter right. However, the more faults are present when an inspector receives an item, the more probable it is that he will miss some of them. It is the elimination of causes of faults that is the hallmark of effective quality control, not their rectification once they have occurred.

Discussion with the responsible executives will soon reveal what the company's attitude to quality is, and how they attempt to assure it. It is also usually worth looking at the inspection reports at various stages of manufacture to find out the number and nature of faults which are being discovered. Unless the product is very highly specialized, it is usually possible to make a judgement about whether the finished quality is reasonably high and likely to be acceptable in the company's chosen market.

Summary

A study of the manufacturing facilities of a business indicates whether or not it is likely to produce products of adequate quality at a low enough cost to allow the company to price competitively and make adequate profits. A well run and efficient factory will not in itself allow a company to be successful, but it will give a company much greater freedom in developing its marketing and product policies. It is also an important resource which must be carefully investigated in order to determine whether it could be used more effectively or possibly adapted for some alternative purpose if the objectives of the profit plan are to be achieved.

Chapter Eleven

FINANCIAL MANAGEMENT

An assessment of the financial management of a company has two general purposes. One is to make sure that the company's financial records give a fair picture of what the company has achieved in the past and what it is currently worth. The other purpose is to find out whether the management control system enables the company's managers to take valid decisions concerning financial matters, and are able to monitor the results of such decisions.

As the accounts of every company are regularly audited by professional accountants, it may seem an unnecessary step in an appraisal of profit potential to consider how far the audited figures are valid. Nevertheless it is a necessary precaution. It is most unlikely that there will be factual errors in audited accounts, or that there will be internal inconsistencies in the figures. However, the basic assumptions may be substantially in error.

Evaluation of assets

The valuation of stocks, for example, is always a matter of judgement. The usual convention is that they should be valued at the lower of market value or cost. However, an auditor cannot be expert in the business of every company whose accounts he audits. He will, therefore, tend to accept the company's own assessment of the market value of stocks.

He will normally examine the rate of turnover of stock and question any items that have been in stores more than a predetermined length of time. Then, depending on the answers he gets, he may reduce the book value of any stock that appears to be in excess of the company's probable requirements. He will, however, rarely be in a position to query, from a commercial viewpoint, stock items which do not reveal a quantifiable reason for suspicion.

It often happens that a company has large stocks of particular items which, although not necessarily slow moving, are valued far above their real market worth.

For instance, one manufacturer of mobile cranes had in stock large numbers of components for models which were about to become obsolete because of a sharp reduction in market demand for that particular type of machine. To an auditor, the stocks were not particularly high compared with past manufacturing rates for the machines in question and, therefore, it seemed quite reasonable to value the stock of components at their cost. In practice, the stocks, which represented an appreciable proportion of the company's net assets, were practically worthless.

To give a more general example, in clothing manufacture fabric designs may become outmoded due to changes in fashion, without this being in any way apparent to an auditor, however conscientious.

The valuation of stocks and work-in-progress is not a process that admits definitive measurement. An estimate of market value is a subjective assessment. Normally, in the case of finished goods, it is easy to form such an assessment for a company's main product range, but much more difficult in the case of such items as spare parts for products in service, or components and raw materials.

When a company suddenly shows substantial losses after a financial year during which the signals appeared to be favourable, this almost always arises because of a stock shortfall revealed at the time of stocktaking. Even worse, when this happens it is often found that the situation has existed for several years undetected, not because of any negligence on the part of the company's auditors, but because the reason for a proportion of the stock becoming valueless has only then become apparent to anyone without a detailed knowledge of the company's market situation.

In any assessment of profit potential it is therefore essential to know how stocks, work-in-progress and other assets have been valued. It is necessary to question basic assumptions behind audited figures, not because of reservations about the professionalism of the audit, but from the knowledge that figures can be based on deceptive information. The particular matters for examination are, among others:

1 The methods employed to value stock and work-in-progress.
2 The valuation of all other assets.
3 Recent or forecast changes in product or market mix which may render plant, tools or materials obsolete within the normal write-down periods.

Product mix

Apart from the effect of changes in product or market mix on the value of plant, stocks of materials, or finished goods, such changes may change the trends of profitability for other reasons.

Many companies do not know with any worthwhile precision what level of profits are being earned by individual items of their product range. There can, therefore, be a real risk that changes in product mix may cause, or may even have already caused, changes in profitability which have not yet been identified. It may also be that a favourable profit trend shown in the accounts has been caused by a fortuitous change in product mix due to (perhaps temporary) changes in market demand.

In one sense, all such changes in market demand are fortuitous, because no company really controls its market; but detecting a change of trend and then planning a product range or defining a pricing policy to exploit the trend, is a sign of inherent strength of management; whereas riding a trend that happens to favourably influence the company's performance, provides a temporary advantage that may disappear with its cause still unrecognized.

Management information

The form of management accounts is important. As has been indicated in Chapter Five, the items considered significant enough to form a basis of routine reports can provide a useful indication of management attitudes. If inadequate data is circulated, then this indicates that the company as a whole is out of control, and is obviously a warning sign to a potential investor. At the other extreme, if each executive is provided with a mass of detail within which it is difficult to separate what is really important from the trivial, this may be an indication that there is a management team which finds it very hard to see the wood from the trees, or one which is industriously churning over detail because it lacks the courage or determination to deal with major issues. If an executive is provided not only with details concerning expenditure and revenue which are under his own control, but also with a great deal concerning matters which he does not control, then this may indicate a lack of clarity in defining responsibilities and organizational structure.

The extent of management information available and its relevance to the needs of each individual executive is, therefore, an indicator of underlying management attitudes. It may not be conclusive, but it does provide pointers for further investigation.

Exploratory questions

There are some general questions to be explored which will help build a pattern of the company's financial strengths and the effectiveness with which it is controlled.

Are the assets of the company realistically represented in the balance sheet?

With regard to land and buildings, it is necessary to know when they were last professionally valued. It is relatively rare to find them overvalued, but it is very common to find the reverse situation; they are included in the balance sheet at the value established many years before and, therefore, are appreciably undervalued. If this is the case, the company concerned may be an attractive acquisition if that is the purpose of the assessment. If, however, the assessment is being carried out by an existing management team it is essential that they should know the real value of the assets they are employing, otherwise any calculation of rate of return on assets employed will be misleading.

In the case of plant and machinery, it is necessary to check whether or not the formula by which its value has been depreciated is valid. In most situations, if a company is equipped with general-purpose plant (wood-working machinery, or sewing machines, for example) then the use of a general depreciation formula is usually acceptable. If, however, the company has a substantial proportion of special-purpose plant, then depreciation according to a formula may be unacceptable; the useful life of the plant may be limited by the market life of the end product, rather than the obsolescence or wear and tear of the plant itself.

The question of valuation of stocks and work-in-progress has been discussed earlier, but apart from questioning the assumptions by which stocks have been valued and the probable life cycle of the end products, it is often advisable to examine a random sample of specific items. Such an examination would consider qualitative factors such as:

1 What is the condition of the stock?
2 What product is it used on?
3 Are the sales of that product likely to continue into the indefinite future; if not, when will they decline?
4 Has it any general market value, or would it have to be scrapped if the product became obsolete.
5 What proportion of its book value could be obtained from the scrap market?

These are general questions. Specific situations will call for a different range of questions, but the principle is the same, which is to find out what factors would affect the value of the items sampled and to form a view as to whether the book value, on average, takes a fair account of such qualitative factors.

Are the assets of the company being used effectively?

The underemployment of assets may represent an opportunity to improve performance or to release working capital for other purposes. It may also reveal a management weakness; one inference could be that there is an opportunity to substantially improve profitability under new management, but that low performance will continue under the existing one.

As so often, there is no absolute guideline that can be adopted. A critical examination of the ratios between turnover and the various forms of assets will provide useful information. Comparative figures can be obtained from published information on other companies, from Government statistics and from the company's own past performance. It is dangerous to rely too much on information about other companies, because the differences in accountancy practice and differences, for example, in make-or-buy policies, can have an appreciable effect on the key ratios, which therefore will not necessarily reflect differences in underlying efficiency.

If there is an adverse trend in the ratio of inventory to turnover which has persisted for some time, it is obviously important to find out why this has occurred.

The best way to go about this is to calculate from first principles the stocks that are really necessary to sustain the business on a sound basis, and the level of creditors and debtors necessary in the company's particular business circumstances.

Have adequate provisions been made in the accounts for process and product replacement or renewal?

In Chapter Nine it was said that there was a need to make sure that the company had a well organized process for product renewal. The cost of such a process, which is necessary to safeguard future profits, must be borne out of current profitability. The disastrous consequences of capitalizing product development costs is exemplified by the recent crisis in the Rolls Royce Aero Engine enterprise. The treatment of development costs in the accounts is therefore a matter for investigation.

There is a similar need to make sure that key processes are also subjected to review and renewal. In this case it can often be quite appropriate to charge the renewal cost as a capital expenditure; the danger may be that inadequate reserves are being put aside for this purpose. If plant has been bought five or ten years earlier and depreciation has been based on its purchase price, it is almost certain this will not cover the eventual replacement cost. Even if some formal system of accounting for inflation is not in use, it is necessary to investigate whether the cash flows will be adequate to permit the plant to be replaced at the right time and to estimate whether profits will still be adequate after taking into account the increased amount of capital employed after plant replacement.

Are profit margins known in appropriate detail and accuracy?

For marketing and pricing purposes it is essential to know product manufacturing costs. If a product is being manufactured regularly over an appreciable period, standard costs are usually required. In other cases it is desirable to know estimated costs and compare them with the actual costs.

In some businesses the overhead cost element includes only variable overheads. In others it includes an apportionment of the fixed overheads of manufacturing, but not the costs of administration or sales functions, and in other cases it may include an apportionment of all overheads. It is not the intention in this book to take a view about the choice between various forms of cost accounting, except to say that a suitable system must be in operation and its strengths and weaknesses must be understood by anyone using it for any purpose, particularly for pricing. The important matter is that the costing system enables management to discriminate between individual parts of the product range, and that the allocation of fixed costs is done in the most meaningful way possible, taking into account the company's business situation. It must be possible to say with confidence, under an identified convention, how much profit is being produced by individual product groups.

If a suitable costing system is in operation, then it is possible to examine the profitability of the individual parts of the product range and, where appropriate, of individual products, and to find out how sensitive the company's profit ability is to changes in product mix. If cost information is not available in sufficient detail to indicate the profitability of each distinct product or product group, then there is danger that one or more product groups may be unprofitable, and a need for a deeper investigation into product profit margins.

Is there budgetary control in operation?

The lack of a system of budgetary control of 'fixed' costs is an indication of weakness in management control and is therefore an adverse indicator of management competence. If such a system does exist, then it is useful to examine the extent of variances and to find out what action has been taken, in the past, to correct adverse ones. If the variances are reported period after period without action apparently being taken to correct them, then the company has a reporting system but not budgetary control. For control, the information must be used to remedy departures from the budget.

The degree to which attention is paid to variances and the efforts which are made to correct them for the future are therefore indicators of the effectiveness of budgetary control and of management concern for profitability.

Are there monthly operating statements?

Most big companies have monthly operating statements that compare actual performance with standard, forecast, or budgeted values. Many small companies still do not have such systems. A company operating without such a system may easily be producing very satisfactory profits, but it is

vulnerable to market changes and may experience a sudden
profit decline because of an adverse trend not identified early
enough.

Each executive needs to receive the minimum amount of information to do his job effectively. Normally he should get information about the revenues and expenditures under his own
direct control, presented in the simplest form compatible with
his needs, and including no redundant information. An executive who has inadequate information cannot manage effectively. On the other hand, one who is swamped with
information may be individually capable of managing well,
but is likely to waste time scanning irrelevant information.

How closely is the budgeting process linked with the long-range planning process?

As indicated earlier, a company's profit potential is normally
evaluated by preparing long- and medium-term profit plans,
then attempting to assess whether or not the plans are likely to
be achieved, and forming a view about the possible extent of
departures from the plans. As the results achieved by a company are usually not compared with the profit plan but with
the budget, it is important that the budgeting process and the
planning process are linked in a meaningful way.

It is not appropriate to treat long-range planning just as an
extension of budgeting. The purpose of the two processes is
different. A profit plan will often include a number of features
which are, by their nature, not capable of precise evaluation. It
may, for example, be decided to purchase a series of distribution outlets. Obviously the timing depends on opportunity and the length of the negotiating process. The profit
plan may include provision for acquisitions, based on the assumption that a certain number of opportunities will arise and
that an estimated proportion of them will be brought to a successful conclusion. A budget must deal only with matters that
are reasonably concrete and, therefore, each acquisition would
be included in the budget only after it had taken place.

There are many examples of this type, which differentiate
between the purpose of a budget and the purpose of a profit

plan. However, the two must be linked because otherwise the plan becomes a paper exercise with no bearing on reality.

The link may be in the organization of the budgeting and the profit planning processes. It may be in the content of a profit plan and the budget, and it may be in their timing. Perhaps, for example, the profit plan is prepared for—say—five years in the future and then the budget is prepared as a development of the first year of the profit plan.

Different companies have different requirements in this respect, depending on the markets in which they are operating, the degree to which growth is based on organic development of existing business or on the acquisition of new businesses, the probability of any given development producing a saleable product, and many other factors. In the assessment of profit potential it is therefore necessary to examine the linkages that exist and decide whether or not they are appropriate to the needs of the particular business.

Summary

An examination of the financial accounts and balance sheet of a business is the traditional method of evaluating a potential acquisition or investment. The theme of this book is that this alone presents too limited a picture, and to form a worthwhile appreciation of a company's future potential one must look beyond the balance sheet. Nevertheless, it is an essential part of an appraisal to ensure that the balance sheet does represent a fair picture of the company's assets and that there is adequate financial control, taking into account each company's unique circumstances. The form of control can provide a useful understanding of the management's attitude towards their business.

Chapter Twelve

LOSS SITUATION

Sometimes an appraisal of profit potential has to be carried out in a company that is losing money. If the rate of loss is relatively low, then an appraisal can take much the same form as the study of a profitable company. If, on the other hand, a company is in a severe loss situation, then there are special factors which must be taken into account.

Time scale of recovery

Every day that passes, more of the company resources are being used up. Obviously, if this continues, the point of no return will eventually be reached and the company will no longer be capable of recovery from its own resources; or of justifying the sums of money which would be necessary from external sources. In a situation of this kind, an accurate estimate of the time scale of profit growth is of more than usual importance.

It will not make a great deal of difference to the long-term viability of a soundly based company if an increase is postponed by, say six months, due to an error in the forecast or because of unforeseen circumstances. In the case of a loss-making company, on the other hand, a similar delay may make the company insolvent and therefore not a worthwhile investment at all.

A very difficult judgement has to be made when an initial appraisal indicates that more money is required in order to tide a company over a period of losses because, if the company does not recover as anticipated, the additional funds will probably have to be written off, and the losses will be higher than if no attempt had been made to recover the situation by injecting the funds.

In this situation, a much more rigorous study of all forecasts must be made (particularly those related to sales volume, because this is usually the key to such a recovery); where there is inadequate data it is best to err on the side of pessimism. Management will usually be under great pressure, both because the company's owners will be requiring an improved performance, and because the managers' own careers will be at risk. They will therefore be more than usually inclined to accept an optimistic view of the situation, to rely too heavily on trends which appear to be favourable to them, and to disregard adverse trends.

There is a further risk that, even if they do not deceive themselves into taking a more favourable view than is justified by all the circumstances, they may tend to present too favourable a picture to a potential investor, whom they may regard as a likely saviour of the business.

Use of a cut-off point

It may be that there is inadequate evidence to support a really confident judgement. Perhaps, for example, the company is about to introduce a new range of products which the sales department believe will be very acceptable to the market-place, and which seem to be well-designed. Despite this, doubts remain; it may be that the products are good but the company's past reputation for product quality is in question. Perhaps the products themselves are complex, so that it is almost certain that some teething troubles will arise and the questions are: How serious will they be? What harm will they do to sales? How quickly can they be resolved when they do arise?

In such a situation, deliberately to take a pessimistic view may be to conclude automatically that profit recovery will not take place, and yet, if the potential return is high compared with the cost of investment, to take such a view may well mean missing a potentially attractive opportunity.

Dilemmas of this kind are, of course, very common in business life. In this acute form probably the best way to deal with it is to decide the minimum rate of profit recovery that would be acceptable, and then to treat this as the cut-off decision point. This minimum recovery rate would normally be lower than the one included in the corporate plan, but usually not as bad as the most pessimistic forecast. If the rate of recovery falls below this curve, then all further investment is stopped and the project or business concerned is closed down, or continued on a low key, depending on judgement about the possibilities of minimizing losses.

The use of such a predetermined and then rigorously enforced cut-off point is easy to consider in abstract terms, but difficult to carry out in practice. There is always a great temptation to invest just a little more because a turning point seems to be in sight, and then some more because having spent so much it is difficult to turn back. So it goes on, until the eventual loss is substantially more than it need have been. Despite the old adage about cutting losses and running profits, many managers succomb to the temptation to do the reverse.

Cash flow

Another feature of a loss situation is that a serious shortage of funds in itself inhibits a company's recovery. The managers spend a great deal of their time dealing with creditors, trying to obtain material supplies, and juggling with available funds in order to keep the business going. All this management time could better be used to tackle the root causes of the profit problem.

There is also the problem that, in a manufacturing situation, batch sizes may often have to be reduced to avoid tying up resources in stocks. As a result, manufacturing costs may be substantially increased due to excessive batch start-up costs.

The timing of the injection of funds is therefore important.

The usual practice is to keep the loss-making business starved of money, providing cash only when the situation is quite desperate, when not to do so would close the business. This is done on the assumption that if funds may be lost in the long term, keeping the company short of money will minimize the risk, and also provoke management to turn the business round quickly.

This can be the wrong approach. It is better to make an objective appraisal and if it is considered that the business has a worthwhile recovery potential, to put in the necessary funds early, so that management can concentrate on dealing with the underlying business problems. Of course, in doing this, all the normal ways of improving cash flow would be considered, and obviously cash flow would still be a central management preoccupation; but with adequate funds it could embark on a systematic programme of improvement and not a series of fire-fighting exercises.

In a loss situation, short- and medium-term cash flow forecasts must be available. The expenditure shown on these must be based on a systematic analysis of the commitments a company has entered and, therefore, the dates by which the money must be paid. For such a purpose it is necessary, for example, to analyse all buying orders in order to estimate when the money will be payable and to consider systematically all other necessary payments. Similarly, the probable cash inflows must be examined taking care not to assume a more optimistic outcome than the situation really justifies. A generalized forecast based on trends would be quite unsatisfactory.

Once the cash flow forecast is available, it becomes possible to decide whether additional funds will be required and, if so, how much will be needed. Normally it is wise to take a pessimistic view of requirements; it may be difficult to get a second injection of cash if it appears that the first has been unsuccessful.

Obviously all the standard methods of reducing the cash requirements will be explored. The obvious means are:

1 Reduction of inventory—with the proviso that taking this too far may be counter-productive.

2 More stringent control of credit.
3 Rigorous limitation of non-essential recruitment and of any avoidable costs.

It is assumed that the company would automatically stretch its own credit-worthiness to the limit. Also, in the extreme case, a redundancy programme would be considered, but this does not usually result in short-term savings and should be avoided if possible.

In summary, therefore, the cash flow forecast is a document of crucial importance and warrants careful study, particularly with regard to the method by which it has been built up.

Supplier reactions

Another matter to be explored is the degree to which the company's suppliers are aware of the situation and are therefore beginning to change their attitude towards the company. Some suppliers may well start to demand payment in advance; others may limit credit to their normal terms of business, in spite of the fact that they have not insisted on this in the past. This may mean that a company that has stretched its credit to an average of five or six months, suddenly finds that it is expected, not just to improve the situation progressively, but to make an immediate and substantial improvement to a level even better than normal.

It may be very difficult to resist such pressures because suppliers have the ultimate sanction of withdrawing supply. Some suppliers may be so dependent on the company that such a threat may only be bluff, but this will not be the normal case. If only one supplier decides to take firm action, less cash will be available for other payments. This could trigger action by other suppliers, and so cause a chain of events which could lead to eventual failure. During appraisal, therefore, it is necessary to find out how close the company is to this situation. A study of recent correspondence with major suppliers, and a check on how many are holding back supplies, will usually provide the necessary information. A change of ownership may eliminate this risk if the new owner is a substantial and reputable company, but may well exacerbate the situation if the new owner is relatively unknown to the creditor companies.

Market reactions

In the market-place, similar risks exist with customers. There can be a great reluctance to buy any except the simplest products from companies thought to be in danger of liquidation. This is quite natural, because a complex product, a piece of engineering equipment for instance, may require regular servicing and the provision of spare parts for many years. Any risk that this service may not be forthcoming is enough to put off any sensible buyer.

A market reaction is perhaps more difficult to discern than in the case of suppliers, because if customers are asked why they are not placing orders they very rarely give an honest answer. Usually they say it is a matter of price or delivery, or refer to particular product features; it is much easier to do that than to say 'we have heard a rumour that you are nearly bankrupt'. Any sign of drying up of orders, therefore, must be taken very seriously and immediate steps taken to reassure customers, if indeed there is anything to reassure them about.

Morale

Nothing harms morale more within a company, particularly at middle and lower management level, than the knowledge that the company is losing money. All employees begin to feel insecure and start looking around for other opportunities. The best people usually have little difficulty in finding other jobs, so there is an appreciable risk that, if losses have continued for some time, the individuals who are needed to promote the recovery may have already moved elsewhere. Even if they have not done so, they may have taken a number of initiatives to secure new jobs, so that even when a recovery programme is in hand they may receive offers which cause them to leave.

If morale is low, there is also the problem that operating standards tend to decline, people tend to start behaving in less co-operative ways. This is natural if they are beginning to become bothered about their own security and perhaps have come to believe that the company will not recover. In an appraisal of recovery potential it is therefore necessary to explore the problems of morale at all levels, but particularly in the management groups. It may be necessary to make management changes just to restore morale if it is found that it has deteriorated to an appreciable extent.

Original causes

The factors that caused the company to fall into a loss-making situation must be ascertained. It is unlikely that there will be only a single cause, although a single cause may be put forward by management. What usually happens is a whole complex of misjudgements and some lack of control; perhaps the pricing strategy was wrong and the financial control system failed to indicate that certain product groups were being sold at a loss; perhaps the products were designed at too high a cost; or manufacturing was inefficient; it may be that management just did not have enough information to control the business. Different managers will give different reasons, but whatever the reasons, serious weaknesses in management must be considered a possibility and, therefore, the management study should be thorough.

Contrasting the loss situation with a favourable prognosis, the question must be asked 'what has happened to change the situation?'. A major change requires equally major causes, therefore if the company has not changed in a readily identifiable way, it is unlikely that a favourable profit forecast will be achieved. A recovery from a bad loss position that does not entail major changes in policy and also changes in the management team is, to say the least, unusual.

Trend indicators

As has been indicated earlier, in a recovery situation the most important factor is the time scale of recovery. It is therefore necessary to monitor the trend of recovery closely to ensure that the programmed rate of improvement is being achieved. For this purpose the company's normal accounts may be inadequate because they are prepared too long after the event. It is often better to select a few key variables which are known to have a major effect on the company's performance, and to obtain reports comparing these key variables with target, at relatively short intervals, and as soon as possible after the events to which they refer.

The choice of the key variables will depend on the business concerned. One may be 'daily value of orders received' or 'goods sold or dispatched'. In any business with a known limited capacity it may be the 'load factor' that is the key variable; this is particularly true of service businesses, where there is no such thing as a finished stock. Whatever the business, it is usually possible to choose not more than about half a dozen separate variables that would give a very good guide to the over-all business trend. The use of these to monitor performance is often a wise precaution, particularly if the decision to continue with the business is a borderline one.

Summary

In a severe loss situation it is necessary to be more than usually careful about the predicted timing of recovery, and to evaluate the attitudes of the company's suppliers and customers, before making a decision about whether or not funds should be made available to finance a recovery programme. If an investment is justified, then it is usually sensible to make adequate funds available early, rather than only in dire necessity. It is also advisable to monitor progress with some care to avoid wasting money if the recovery trend does not develop at the forecast rate.

For a variety of reasons, an appraisal of a loss-making company is more than usually critical, and more than usually difficult. The only rule is that recovery almost always takes longer than management think it will take, and the temptation to throw good money after bad afflicts otherwise hard-headed businessmen to an unexpected degree.

Chapter Thirteen

ASSESSING RISK

In evaluating a potential investment, shrewd investors pay at least as much attention to the risk of loss as they do the possibility of profit. The reason is not hard to see: it is a difficult process to obtain a return on investment much greater than 15 per cent (discounting inflationary factors), but it is extremely easy to lose 100 per cent. An investment that fails may potentially use up all the profits, in the same year, of six good investments. On the other hand, if the investment is one in which most of the capital is secure, then even if the project is unsuccessful, the average return from all investments will not be much affected.

There is, therefore, a good reason for looking very closely at what happens in the investment is unsuccessful. There are two factors involved:

1 The reliability of the various assumptions which support the profit forecast.
2 The sensitivity of profit level to errors in those assumptions.

Reliability of assumptions

In building up any forecast, there are certain figures that the forecaster knows are relatively firm, and others in which, however much care is taken, there is an appreciable element of personal judgement not very well supported by objective measurement. These areas of relative strength and weakness vary from one forecast and one company to another.

In one situation it may be the sales forecast that is reliable, and manufacturing output or unit cost that is difficult to forecast accurately. An example of this would be a company relocating its factories because of labour shortages. There might be considerable doubts about the time required for the move, the rate at which raw labour could be recruited and trained, and the quality of output during the training period.

During the launch of a new product, particularly if it is similar to products the company is already making, the opposite situation may apply in which the manufacturing cost can be forecast with considerable confidence, but the market forecast is in doubt.

The profit forecast may rely on improvements in performance (such as the reduction in unit cost of a product, or of various overhead costs), upon the disposal of part of a business, or on the development of new product ranges within a specified time scale. The confidence with which any of these events can be forecast will obviously vary considerably from one case to another.

In any given situation it is therefore necessary to rank factors that influence the profit forecast, according to the estimated degree of confidence. A typical ranking table might look rather like Figure 13.1.

In this example the areas where there is low confidence in the precision of the forecast are: the sales forecast of product group B, because this is a new group about to be launched; and the profit margin on product group C, because there is a target to reduce costs by 10 per cent in the face of price competition.

In constructing such a table, all the main elements of the forecast should be included and for each element the definition of high, low and medium degrees of confidence should be established by approximate benchmarks.

It should be emphasized that what is in question is not the absolute level of the forecast under review, which was settled when the profit plan was prepared, but the strength of the supporting evidence for the forecast. *High* means that there is a

Item	Confidence	Remarks
Sales forecast:		
Product Group A	High	Well established products
Product Group B	Low	New product launch
Product Group C	Medium	Increasing competition
		met with price reductions
. . . .		
Margins:		
Product Group A	High	Considerable past data
Product Group B	Medium	Good detailed estimates
Product Group C	Low	Aim to reduce cost by 10%
. . . .		
Production output:		
Product Group A	Medium	Shortage of skilled labour –
		training in hand
Product Group B	Medium	Production line still
		learning job
Product Group C	High	Well established group
. . . .		
Works overhead costs	High	Firm data
Sales overhead costs	Medium	Risk of high staff turnover
Administration	High	Firm data
Etc.		

Figure 13.1   Assessment of forecasting confidence

great deal of factual supporting information and that therefore it is most unlikely that the forecast will be in error to any significant degree. *Medium* means that the forecast is supported by some factual data, but reservations exist perhaps because the forecast is contingent on circumstances which are externally controlled or difficult to predict. *Low* indicates that there is an appreciable subjective content in the forecast and an appreciable risk of error.

The purpose of preparing a table of this type is to act as a reminder and a check list. It should not be treated in a mechanistic manner; there is no way of computing such levels of confidence in the real world where time pressures are high and the available facts always sparse. Various statistical techniques could theoretically be used, and no doubt would be used, where appropriate, in preparing the plan originally; but, in the assessment of risk, judgement is required rather than formulae. It is also as well to speculate generally about ways in which a project might be unsuccessful in case these have not been brought out by the check list.

It may seem over pessimistic to dwell on all the things that can go wrong with a project, but to think about the unthinkable early enough, may lead to the avoidance of expensive mistakes.

In this way, the high risk areas in a forecast are highlighted so that they can be given special attention, possibly by the establishment of special monitoring arrangements.

Profit sensitivity

The second factor to be explored is the sensitivity of the profit forecast to variation in performance in the key areas. If a particular product group, for example, is launched six months after forecast date; if a forecast 10 per cent reduction in unit labout cost turns out to be only 4 per cent; if a planned price increase causes an unexpected drop in sales; what will be the effect on profitability?

In considering such matters it is normally necessary to assume that reasonable measures will have been taken to contain the effect. If, for example, there is a shortfall in sales turnover, output will be reduced and the rate of intake of materials adjusted. It is the net effect on profits after all remedial steps have been taken that must be estimated in order to form a balanced judgement about the degree of risk.

Naturally, there is no need to consider such questions of profit sensitivity with respect to all the elements that make up a profit plan. It is normally necessary only for those in which there is a low degree of confidence in the forecast, or where particularly high profit sensitivity is considered likely.

There is no point in attempting to be too precise in such estimates. Most attempts to calculate such factors with precision
are spurious. What is needed is to know the order of the effect,
as part of a total pattern.

Terminal losses

If a project is a borderline one, in which there is thought to be
significant risk of eventual failure, then it is necessary to assess
what would happen if it was decided to close it down. In some
industries the stocks, plant, equipment, buildings, etc., would
be readily saleable at price levels that would have a reasonable
relationship to their book value. In others, closing down
would amount to writing off most of the value tied up in such
items.

As an illustration, if the plant required to manufacture a
product group is a standard range of lathes, milling machines,
grinders and general-purpose equipment of this type, then if
the project goes wrong, it can easily be used for something else.
If, on the other hand the project requires special-purpose
machinery, say a transfer line to machine a complex casting or
a specialized process plant, it is very unlikely that the plant can
be used economically for any other purpose.

The two cases in financial terms may be superficially similar, but the outcome of failure is quite different. In the first
case much of the money may be recovered, in the second
most will be lost.

Similar considerations apply to the building itself. A general-purpose building may be saleable without loss. A special-
purpose building, depending on its precise function, may be
unusable for another purpose or usable only at an economic
disadvantage which reduces its potential value.

One illustration of this is the poor value of a disused
cinema. Some were expensively converted to bowling alleys
which also have a low residual value. Not unnaturally there is
a reluctance on the part of the same investors to put up
squash courts because these too are highly specialized buildings. In this case there may be some protection given by high
site values, but in the case of similarly specialized industrial

buildings such protection will be less likely to arise.

There are, therefore, a range of exploratory questions concerned with the confidence behind the profit plan, sensitivity to errors in the basic assumptions, and the cost of ultimate failure.

Exploratory questions

What is the strength of each of the assumptions which form the foundation for the profit plan?

Each of the assumptions behind the profit plan is considered individually and the evidential support for its validity is examined. This must be done systematically and it can help to use the table referred to earlier, illustrated in Figure 13.1. It is necessary to challenge any evidence presented in order to expose its basic strength.

What would happen if the demand were to fall short of the market forecast by 10 per cent ... 15 per cent ... 20 per cent. . . ?

The question as presented here is, of course, oversimplified. If different product groups are made by separate processes and have different levels of profitability, then it is clearly necessary to ask this question separately for each product group. Properly considered answers will reveal how sensitive is the profitability of the business to variations in market demand. They will also indicate whether or not contingency plans have been made, whether they are appropriate, and whether they are likely to be reasonably effective.

Remedial action in marketing would also obviously be considered, perhaps by the extension of the geographical marketing area, by strengthening various aspects of the marketing mix, or by a change in pricing strategy. If the original plan was well conceived it is likely that each of these would involve additional marketing cost or some reduction in margin and, therefore, would have the effect of reducing profitability.

There might be a need to postpone the manufacturing programme or to reduce the rate of output, or to continue as
planned and hold the products in stock. The effect on profitability and cash flow of taking one or other of these courses
would need to be considered.

**What would happen if the supply of a product was reduced, due to
manufacturing delays or component supply problems, etc., by 10
per cent . . . 15 per cent . . . 20 per cent. . . ?**

As before, it is necessary to consider this question separately
for each product group. Apart from the obvious effect of lack
of profit and overhead contribution from the profit group concerned, there may also be problems because of the inter-
relationship between various product groups in the market-
place. The lack of availability of one product may depress the
sales of other associated products.

Contingency plans may include the possibility of subcon-
tracting, adding additional capacity, starting a double shift, all
of which may add to cost and therefore affect profitability.
There would also presumably be the problem of materials
brought to meet the required programme which will now
represent an excess stock which must be financed and so increase interest charges.

**What would happen if the manufacturing cost of one or more of
the product group is 5 per cent . . . 10 per cent . . . above the estimate?**

If the response is that it is possible to increase the selling price,
then the existing selling price is too low and ought to be increased anyway. If, on the other hand, selling prices cannot be
increased, there is the secondary question: how long will it take
to redesign the product at a lower cost and why has this not
been done already? This question, therefore, amounts to a
challenge to the validity of the existing product cost estimate
and an attempt to find out how soundly based it is. Obviously
it is right that the first response is an attempt to increase prices
or reduce product cost, but this should have been explored as

part of the ongoing process of management and should therefore be already in hand.

Usually it is necessary to modify the product, changing both the price and cost in order to get a better balance between them. If margins are too low, therefore, almost always some product redesign is necessary, with consequent delays and additional development cost.

What would be the effect if the launch of a new product was delayed by three months—six months—nine months. . . ?

A delay due to an over-run in the product development stage would obviously cause a loss of profit contribution; there might also be a build up of stocks of materials called in to meet the original product launch date. There will almost certainly be additional development costs because these are usually time-related costs. There will also presumably be delays in the remainder of the product development programme. Such a delay could therefore cause a considerable shortfall in profitability and could indicate the start of a chain reaction of further delays.

What happens if there is a labour shortage in certain key trades?

It is necessary to know how far a labour shortage would prevent production reaching its planned level or whether remedial action could be taken. This could include the institution of a training programme, arrangements for the work to be subcontracted to a factory in another area where there are fewer labour difficulties, or the redesign of the product to reduce the need for the particular labour category in short supply. All of these would cause delays, take up management time and cost money; all of them therefore have an effect on profitability.

What would be the effect if overhead costs are above the planned level?

Much depends on the reason for the excess cost and whether it is part of the fixed or variable element of the overheads. An excessive rate of variable overheads is particularly harmful because the improvement in volume does not counteract it. If this is the problem and the variable overhead level is regarded as being irreduceable, the pricing and direct cost elements must be examined with the object of improving margins, in order to avoid a direct drain on profitability.

If fixed overheads are too high and cannot be reduced, obviously one possibility is to increase volume; this may entail extra cost in market development, and possibly the cost of product modifications to meet new market requirements.

The effect of excessive overhead costs can therefore appear as a direct drain on profitability or indirectly through extra expenditure on marketing, product redesign, etc.

What would be the effect if certain specified executives were to leave the company immediately after an investment or merger?

A response to this question might be that they cannot leave because they are under contract; which is all very well as far as it goes, but it is very hard to hold a man and get him to carry out effective work if he wants to leave. There is also the problem of departure through illness or accident.

A surprising number of projects depend, to a very high degree, on the competence, knowledge or the skill of a very small group of executives, sometimes just one man. It is a truism to say that no man is irreplaceable, but, in practice, in the short term many men are almost so. A project that is highly dependent on a few individuals must therefore be regarded as being at least in the moderate risk category. The departure of such individuals may temporarily halt the growth or development of the business without causing any depletion of funds already in the business; on the other hand it may cause a very serious setback.

An obvious example of this is in the couture business where success often depends very much on one person. In industry in general the problem is not usually so acute, but there are many circumstances in which the sudden departure of the key salesman, an engineering designer, a chemist, may have very serious repercussions on the short-term future of a business. The departure of the man at the top can also be a source of threatening problems, particularly if there has not been adequate provision in the company's plan for management succession.

What happens if an investment in a new project fails?

As asked here, this question is of course too general. There can be various causes of failure, some of which have been raised in earlier questions and these will have differing effects on the probable outcome. It is, however, necessary to think about the consequences of failure in terms of security of the investors' funds.

Usually, for any new project, funds will be required for:

1 New product development.
2 Prototype manufacture and testing.
3 Financing production plant.
4 Providing factory space.
5 Financing stocks of raw materials and components.
6 Initial sales promotion.
7 Stocks in the distribution chain.
8 Losses during the market development phase.
9 Etc.

Some of these items would obviously be lost entirely if the project were unsuccessful; for example, product and market development costs would not be recoverable. Other costs, such as the expenditure on raw material and components, and the stocks of finished products, will have a residual value which will obviously be less than their value as part of an ongoing project, but the percentage of the money expended which can be recovered will vary between extremes.

Certain kinds of raw material have a very high intrinsic value so that, if a project is abandoned, most of the material can be sold almost at its cost price. A jewellery manufacturer using precious metals would be in this situation, as to a lesser degree would be a manufacturer using tin and copper as major material items. In the case of other components or materials, resale value may be very low. Iron or steel castings, for instance, especially if they have been machined, offer scrap values which represent only a very small percentage of the cost. Fabrics of various kinds offer varying resale possibilities. There is, indeed, almost an infinite range of conditions. Every case needs special examination and individual assessment.

Expenditure on plant and buildings is also potentially recoverable and again a proportion which can be recovered is variable from one project to another.

Summary

If a company's performance begins to depart from the profit plan, the managers of the company will usually be working very hard to put matters right. In spite of this, sometimes it is not possible to rectify the situation and there may be an appreciable loss of profitability, possibly leading to an ultimate failure of the business. An essential part of an appraisal of profit potential is therefore to assess the risk of this happening. To do this it is necessary to consider:

1 The likelihood of an error in the forecast.
2 The potential effect of such an error on profitability.
3 The cost of ultimate failure of the business.

This makes it possible to judge the degree of risk, and make an informed decision.

Chapter Fourteen

MERGERS

Companies enter merger negotiations for various reasons. Some have carefully prepared plans for expansion which entail the acquisition of particular marketing, manufacturing or financial strengths. Other companies are seeking growth itself and tend to seize opportunities without necessarily being concerned with fitting them to a general pattern. Therefore, the range of benefits which may be expected by the participants is very wide; it may include any of the following.

Financial

A primary reason is often to increase the parent company's rate of return on capital employed. This can be achieved, for instance, by buying a profitable company at a relatively low multiple of profit earnings because it happens to be in an industry which does not have a glamour rating on the stock exchange; or perhaps buying one with assets that are not being used effectively and which are undervalued in the company's accounts, the intention may be to use the assets more effectively after the acquisition, or merely to sell them to reduce the level of capital employed in the combined business.

If the reason for an acquisition is a purely financial one, without any intention of joint working, some of the special considerations in this chapter would not necessarily apply. Usually, however, there is a mixture of financial and other reasons for any acquisition.

Market development

A company may wish to enter new markets or gain a greater penetration in existing markets; it may be that the company being acquired can bring in new customers for the parent company's products; it may enable it to present a more comprehensive range of products to existing customers. Obviously, the relationship between the old customer group and the new, and the degree to which the product ranges overlap or complement each other, will vary greatly from case to case.

Technical

A company may wish to enter a new technical field in which it is not currently competent to operate. It may therefore decide to buy a company which already has the necessary competence rather than to build up its own expertise in the field. It may believe that its own marketing, management, and financial strengths are such that it can exploit the technical competence more successfully than the company it is acquiring.

Manufacturing

A merger may be initiated with the objective of combining the manufacturing resources of two companies in order to make economies in the use of space, or plant, or to get longer production runs. There may also be the possibility of reducing the combined overhead costs by having a single management team and administrative system. If the product ranges overlap the rationalization of the combined range may achieve manufacturing economies.

Management

A company may be acquired because of its management

strengths, sometimes because it is intended to use them to rejuvenate the parent company. On the other hand, it may be acquired because of weaknesses in its management, in the belief that the acquiring company can produce a rapid profit turnround by the injection of such strengths.

There are obviously many other benefits that could be sought by merger or acquisition and usually the aim is to gain a combination of several benefits. By considering the reasons for a particular merger, it may be broadly classified as horizontal, vertical or conglomerate.

Horizontal mergers arise when both the companies concerned are selling similar products to similar customers. There may be considerable product overlap, but usually the combined range will be wider than either of the individual ones. There may also be common customers, but in most cases the market segment of the combined company will be larger than either of the companies individually.

Sometimes the product ranges or technologies of the two companies are appreciably different and the purpose of the merger is to be able to combine the marketing aspects of the two businesses and so provide customers with a more complete range of products or services. In other cases it is the technology of the two companies that is to be merged, and the basic reason for the acquisition is to add new marketing strengths, perhaps in a new geographic area or a new market segment. Such mergers are often referred to as concentric mergers.

The purpose of a horizontal merger is, therefore, usually to obtain a higher rate of return on investment by rationalizing marketing, development, or manufacturing strengths. Allied to this is often the desire to protect an existing market situation from competitive aggression, by offering a wider range of products.

Vertical mergers are those in which a company buys one or more of its customers or suppliers. In the first case, this is usually part of a plan to obtain greater profitability by obtaining a reasonably stable base demand and thereby minimizing demand fluctuations. If the acquired company is a supplier, then the purpose may be to secure a reliable source of supply of an essential material or product. In both cases there is the

implication that the two companies can save buying and selling costs at the interface between the two operations, and both
can plan more rational inventories.

Conglomerate mergers, now becoming less fashionable than
they were in the early sixties, occur when a company is
acquired which has no similarity in products, markets or technology with its parent. The intention behind the merger may
be to buy a high rate of return on investment, or management
competence, or assets, but it is not expected that operationally
there will be any significant merger of activities.

These three kinds of mergers obviously have different implications for management, both in terms of pre-appraisal investment and subsequent organization and control.

Merger problems

An appraisal of profit potential carried out before the merger
of two companies, or before the acquisition of one company by
another, poses special problems. These problems have their
roots in the problems of the mergers themselves. It is perhaps
unsafe to generalize on such a complex subject, but generally if
a merger is to be successful, one or both of the companies
involved must experience a considerable change in its corporate life style. Yet, before the merger, both parties often
seem to believe, or behave as if they believe, that their own
management style, form of organization and methods of
working will be retained in the merged entity.

This problem arises partly because during the discussions
that lead up to the merger the executives on both sides who are
in favour of the merger will be presenting to their colleagues all
the favourable aspects, and reassuring them about their
doubts and reservations. Amongst the senior managers
involved there may also be a certain amount of self-deception;
they may allow themselves to see only the favourable aspects
of the merger and turn a blind eye to the problems. Lower
down in the companies concerned, there is likely to be much
less support, and even if the merger is obviously logical taking
into account the company's circumstances, there may be personal feelings of insecurity which may harden into defensive

opposition to change, after the merger.

Plainly, if a merger is to be successful in the sense that the performance of the combined companies is to be better than the sum of the performance of the two companies separately, then methods of operating must change in ways which are not necessarily foreseeable at the time the merger is discussed.

If the projected merger is between two companies that are roughly equal in size, then the problems of achieving a successful merger are intensified. There are many examples of companies which have merged together to obtain the benefits of rationalizing markets, products, manufacturing and financial strengths and yet very little rationalization is achieved after the merger. The two companies continue to exist side by side, sharing little else except common shareholders and a token merger of top management.

This arises because neither party is managerially strong enough to dominate the other, and neither party will voluntarily relinquish its own established practices in favour of those of its partner. This was the kind of pattern that arose when the Morris and Austin car firms were merged to form the British Motor Corporation. It was only after a long period of decline and the intervention of Leyland as a third and managerially dominant partner that the two units were welded together.

It is reasonable to conclude that a merger between two companies is likely to be successful only if it is, in management terms, a takeover of one company by another. Goodwill is not a sufficiently powerful force to overcome innate resistance to change. The feeling that 'my tribe is better than your tribe' is not easily set aside. For success there must normally be a dominant partner.

Need for a full appraisal

The very wide variety of reasons for which mergers are undertaken and the complex nature of the interactions which are likely after the merger make it essential that a detailed systematic appraisal takes place before final agreement is reached.

During the negotiation stage, there is bound to be discussion about how the merged companies are to be operated. It is easy, if information is inadequate, to make promises that cannot be kept when the full facts are known. If, after the merger when more information is known, the promises are broken, then disillusionment can have a very serious effect on performance.

A typical example of this is when the company to be acquired is told that it will remain largely autonomous and then finds, after the merger, that the parent is exercising considerable control of many aspects affecting profitability. It may be that the parent applied control only because it felt that the subsidiary was running into trouble, or perhaps the parent was only paying lip service to the concept of autonomy to get the merger accepted. It may even be that what seems like autonomy to the parent feels like a very tight rein to the subsidiary.

The attitude, which is prevalent, of getting the deal through and worrying about the later management situation afterwards, does not seem to be a wise approach and, generally, a merger will be successful only if there has been absolute integrity by both the parties during the prior negotiations. Even integrity, however, depends on adequate understanding.

It is thus necessary to decide beforehand how an acquisition will be managed in its new environment. Is it to remain largely autonomous, reporting at a high level in the acquiring company? Is it to be substantially merged operationally, or is it to be treated in some way between these extremes? Each possibility will have some relevance to the appraisal in that it will influence the range of factors which have to be considered before a satisfactory conclusion can be drawn. For example, if the two companies are to be closely merged then attention has to be given to the management styles of the two companies. If, on the other hand, the acquired company is to be relatively independent, there is much less need for a close fit in this field.

In most cases a company making an acquisition is attempting to obtain some quality it does not already have and expects, in turn, to supply something to the acquired company which will enable that company to be more profitable. What is important, therefore, is not just how profitable the acquired company will be in its own right, but how well it complements the existing business strengths of the parent. This means, in effect, that both companies must be appraised at least to the extent of getting an understanding of the distinctive competence of both.

For instance, one company started a growth phase very short of cash, but with a lively and intelligent management team. It bought, therefore, in the first instance, companies which were unsuccessful because of management problems. In appraising its acquisitions, it was concerned with market and product strengths, and with the resources of the business, relative to the price it was paying; but poor management in the companies to be acquired was a positive advantage because it enabled them to be bought cheaply. The parent was able to inject this after acquisition and so produce rapid profit growth.

Before many years it had become a very successful company, its profits were high and its cash flow was very healthy but by this time its management was becoming stretched. Its acquisition policy therefore changed steadily until it was looking for companies that were already highly profitable with strong management teams. As its own available resources changed, so did its acquisition needs, so that a company which would have been a highly satisfactory acquisition at one time would have been completely unsatisfactory a relatively short time later.

Acquisition, if it is to be successful, always entails a substantial amount of change in both the acquired company and, to a lesser degree, the parent. One resource, therefore, which is always needed in abundance after a merger is management talent. It is a simple truism that if one inadequately managed company mergers with another one equally under-managed, the result will be, not just to add together the management problems of the two companies, but to multiply them by a considerable factor.

One factor that often causes problems after a merger is an appreciable size mismatch. It was said earlier in this chapter that a merger between two companies of equal size often leads to serious problems. Bearing in mind the problem of management of change, it is probably best if the acquired company is not more than a quarter of the size of the acquiring company. This is a far from absolute rule and every case must be considered on its merits, but if the companies concerned are close together in size, then there is a clear case for a very thorough study of the management of the two companies and very careful decisions about how the combined companies should be managed.

The other extreme situation is when the acquired company is very small compared with its parent. In this case there is often a feeling that, just because it is small, there is no need to bother too much about its management. The truth is that management problems are far from proportional to company size; a small acquisition may cause management problems and soak up management time out of all proportion to the potential benefit arising from the acquisition.

If an acquisition is particularly small, it usually requires a different style of management to the parent. Systems of control necessary in a large business are neither necessary nor suitable in a small one; often the whole benefit of small size is the flexibility that enables a company to react quickly to market changes, and this is almost necessarily lacking in a large company. The imposition of the control system of a large company in such a circumstance may easily eliminate the very strength which was a source of the acquired company's attractiveness as a purchase.

Careful thought about why the company is being acquired can help to minimize the risk of mistakes in later methods of control, but if the acquired company is less than 5 per cent of the size of the parent, there is an appreciable risk that the gap in management style may not be easily bridged.

Crucial factors

In summary, therefore, there are three critical factors in achieving a successful merger:

1 The prospective parent company should have clear understanding of its own distinctive competence. In the light of that knowledge, a specification can be prepared of the kind of company which it could successfully acquire in

order to improve its performance in a defined way. This definition should be adhered to; companies should not be acquired on an opportunistic basis (unless the opportunity happens to fit the defined strategy).

2 Usually, the most difficult problem is the availability of competent managers to deal with the period of change following an acquisition. If these are not available, then the acquisition will almost certainly fail.

3 The form of organization and the reporting procedures must be designed so that they allow management energies to concentrate on the areas where profits are generated. Particularly they must not modify the subsidiary company's ways of working for the sake of uniformity, as to do so might eliminate the very strength that the acquiring company was seeking.

In a potential merger situation, therefore, a number of special considerations must be taken into account:

1 The objectives of a merger must be defined in advance and known before the assessment takes place.

2 A plan in relation to the organization, management, marketing and manufacturing policies of the merged company must be known or prepared in the course of the appraisal, so that there is no misunderstanding about what is intended and how it is to be achieved.

3 The management style of the two companies must be explored and compared.

4 Potential leaders of the combined management team must be identified.

As before, this is best done by asking a number of questions.

Exploratory questions

What is the acquisition strategy of the company initiating the merger?

There should be a written statement of the company's objectives and policy indicating the purposes of its acquisition strategy. It should also define the strengths that the acquiring company is seeking and specify the limits of size, profitability, cost, market and product area of, and subsequent management policies towards, any acquisition.

Such a specification will ensure that any company presented for appraisal is at least, on first analysis, a suitable subject for acquisition and worth the cost of a serious appraisal.

Does the company being appraised fit the defined specification?

If it fits on first examination, then a detailed appraisal is justified. If it does not fit the stated specification, then a secondary question may be asked: Are there any other reasons which are so compelling that the policy should be modified? If there are, then such reasons need very careful consideration to make sure that they really are valid. It is sometimes easy to rationalize the acceptance of a tempting, but nevertheless, unsuitable opportunity.

Does it fit the parent?

A potential acquisition may well conform to the specification but may still not be a good fit with the parent company. This is partly because a specification is a limited statement in a number of key areas, and there may be important qualitative differences in aspects not covered by it. The specification may also be based on a misunderstanding of the acquiring company's strengths and weaknesses and a number of important considerations may therefore have been omitted.

As indicated earlier, what is being sought is a complementary fit; deficiencies can be accepted provided they can be compensated by the potential parent.

Does the management style of the two companies fit?

One of the biggest single causes of failure of mergers is a misfit between the management style of the companies concerned. The most obvious case is when a company with an autocratic management style acquires one in which there has been a substantial amount of participation by all executives in its management decisions. In such a situation, the management team of the acquired company will very soon find jobs elsewhere rather than accept the restraints inherent in the new style.

The opposite situation is equally likely to cause problems. If a management team that is used to being closely controlled is suddenly expected to make a major contribution to policy, individual managers will take time to adjust to the new situation and some will be unable to operate successfully in the changed environment. There may be some who have a psychological need to work for a dominant individual and they may find their new frame of reference quite unsatisfactory.

The degree of control that a company exercises over subsidiaries is, therefore, important, but so also is the kind of control. Some companies are concerned only with the financial management of subsidiaries, and provided that they receive satisfactory operating statements are little concerned with other matters. In other companies there is central control over other functional areas such as personnel management, marketing, manufacturing, engineering and design policies. The degree of control in each of these functions often depends upon the historical mode of development of the parent company and is often not at all related to the needs of the present.

As the parent is unlikely to change, it is necessary to make sure that the subsidiary can accept the kinds of control which are customary within the parent company. In this context, the acceptance of such methods applies not only to the attitude of the management team, but also the company's operating situation. For example, innovation tends not to flourish in a big company and therefore a small subsidiary often should be allowed a good deal of freedom just to preserve its existing performance levels, even if its managers might willingly accept large company disciplines.

Is there enough management talent?

Each of the managers must be appraised in terms of his past achievement, so that an attempt can be made to designate an adequate management team for the combined companies. As a merger is very demanding on management talent, a surplus of strength in this field can be beneficial. Particularly important is identification of who will be the executive concerned with day-to-day management of the affairs of the subsidiary (if it is not to be fully merged) and who will be responsible for it within the parent company. It is obvious that these two individuals must be able to work well together.

Summary

Mergers present special problems and the failure rate is high. It is therefore particularly important that before a merger takes place both the companies concerned are carefully appraised to make sure that the merger is taking place for the right reasons, that the two companies complement each other and that management problems can be effectively solved.

Chapter Fifteen

IDENTIFYING
A PATTERN

In the preceding chapters each aspect of the appraisal has been dealt with separately, but in reality all parts of a company interlock, so that questions relating to one function of the business can often produce answers that have implications in other functions. There is, therefore, a need for cross-reference, not only in formulating the profit plan, but also in carrying out a qualitative assessment of the company's ability to achieve the plan.

For example, decisions about marketing obviously affect production plans. Sales demand may be predicted to increase at a continuous rate, whereas production capacity can normally be increased only in steps. The effect of learning by production operatives delays the full benefit from increasing capacity and, therefore, smooths the rate of increase, but production output will never respond precisely to market demand unless the works are badly underloaded. Therefore, not only does market demand affect production planning, but production capability affects response to market demand. Similarly, both affect the financial plan in terms of cash flows, profitability, capital required for stockholding and other financial matters.

Qualitative factors

Such quantitative links are normally dealt with in the profit plan, but other factors may also have to be considered. These are factors based on informed judgement about a situation, for example consequences of a specific departure from plan may be more widespread than a simple empirical calculation would suggest. For instance, if a company is marketing a product for which there is marked seasonal variation of demand, then a delay of say, one month, in producing a newly developed addition to the product range, may cause the product launch to be delayed by a full year.

Similarly, if there is a risk that a new product will have difficulty in meeting the advertized specification, or may have quality problems, this can have a serious effect on market acceptance. Even if the problems are resolved quickly, the memory of them may remain in customers' minds long after their cause has been eliminated. For reasons of this kind, lack of confidence in quality may cause a product launch to be delayed, or for it to be carried out selectively to market sections considered relatively insensitive to low quality.

For any product there is usually a choice of manufacturing methods determined by the planned production volume, each method becoming the most economical at a different level of output. It is usual to find that the method most economical for high volume tends to be capital-intensive, and the method suitable for low volume tends to be labour-intensive. There may be a situation where the sales volume predicted by the market forecast would justify using the capital-intensive method of manufacture where, however, unit costs would increase rapidly if the plant were to be underloaded.

If there are any serious reservations about the market forecast it may, in such a situation, be better not to choose the capital-intensive method of manufacture, even though it is the best at the planned volume, because it is too sensitive to any volume reduction. The quality of the sales forecast may, therefore, affect the choice of production methods and anticipated production cost. A low quality sales forecast would, in this example, lead to a decision to accept a lower unit profit margin as insurance against the effects of a possible shortfall in demand.

If the company has serious problems of industrial relations, its ability to meet a production programme or to deliver products on time may have to be questioned and the marketing strategy may have to be adjusted to take account of the risk of a shortfall in supply. Any such changes obviously affect cash flow and rate of profitability.

Emergence of a pattern

A company is an organic whole. All the parts must relate to each other and, although a business may well be stronger in some areas than others, it is relatively rare to find a major degree of imbalance. If there is inefficient control, poor morale, a low level of professional competence, or a lack of integrity in any functional area, all the others will be affected. If there appear to be marked differences in the performance of the various sections of the business, it is wise to make sure that these are real and not just due to the way the executives concerned have presented the facts.

There is, therefore, a need for a series of judgements concerning the inter-relation between the different business functions (which may have qualitative as well as quantitative implications) and these together must form a coherent pattern.

Contradictions, or too many conflicting views about the same aspects of the business, usually indicate that the study has not been carried out in sufficient depth, or that probably some of the executives involved have been less than frank.

Of course, there will always be different viewpoints within a business. Some tension and some conflict between individuals is essential in order to generate innovation and change. Individuals may also vary considerably in their interpretation of similar facts. The comparison between the shoe salesman who went to Africa and said 'there is no demand there, nobody wears shoes' and his colleague who said 'the market is wide open, nobody has shoes' is valid in many other situations.

However, despite all the differences of viewpoint, temperament and understanding between the executives concerned, a pattern should emerge if an appraisal has been carried out competently; if it does not, the conflicting points must be re-examined.

It is often useful, if the programme permits, to pause after the questioning stage of an appraisal and to think about the various aspects of the study, to absorb the data and to re-examine any controversial aspects of the business. It is then necessary to answer some very basic questions, such as:

1　What is the distinctive competence of the business?
2　What level of profitability could be achieved in future by fully exploiting that competence?
3　Does the company have adequate resources to implement the profit plan? If not, what additional resources are required? In particular, how strong is the management resource?
4　What is the probability of profitability falling short of the plan? Is it possible to assign upper and lower limits?
5　What would be the cost of failure?

The most important of these fundamental questions, and the one most frequently omitted, is the first question—about the distinctive competence of the business. It is often found that the company is trying to compete in markets to which its strengths are not particularly relevant, or it may believe that its strength is in its technical competence and concentrate on special development work while, in truth, its ability to deliver on time is where its strength lies. In such a case, identification of its distinctive competence will enable the company to develop a new corporate plan seeking growth in fields where its strengths can be exploited.

The second question is concerned with the formulation and validity of the profit plan which were discussed earlier in Chapter Five. The plan may be one that was already available within the company or it may be produced as part of the appraisal. Whichever applies, it needs to be built up by careful judgement from the best available information. The resources too are very important and it is very easy to define a profit plan that outruns the resources of a business, particularly in the case of its management resources; an assessment of the quality and extent of resources is an essential part of any conclusions.

The general probability of the profit plan being achieved

and the risk of loss if there is any significant departure from the plan need to be assessed particularly if additional investment funds are needed, or in a loss situation.

How all this is put together in written form depends a great deal on the purpose of the appraisal. If it is being carried out on behalf of an investor who intends to remain at arm's length, the investigation has to determine how successful the company is likely to be under existing conditions with existing management, but perhaps with extra financial backing. The appraisal, therefore, will be less concerned with developing an action plan.

If, on the other hand, the appraisal is being carried out by a company in the course of its normal business development, then an action plan is an essential part of the appraisal. It becomes necessary to postulate alternative profit plans with different investment costs and different levels of profitability and also to consider the effect and the consequences of a limited range of the most probable contingencies.

If a potential merger is the purpose of an appraisal, the appraisal would concentrate much more on the relationship between the two companies concerned, rather than the absolute levels of performance expected. It would certainly include consideration of the future working relationship between the two management teams and of the degree and kind of control required.

There are many other reasons for an appraisal: a parent company carrying out an appraisal of a subsidiary; a company in more than one business appraising the potential profit from one of its businesses; a company entering a new field; an existing investor trying to decide whether to withdraw loan funds or to lend more money; the examination of business in order to decide whether it should be put into liquidation.

The degree of detail and the emphasis on differing aspects will vary from case to case, but all the information necessary to make a decision must be included.

Nature of conclusions

If the appraisal is being carried out as part of the normal business development process, it will be heavily slanted towards action that has to be taken to ensure that the profit potential is achieved as part of an ongoing process of management with opportunity for further review and modification. In this case the forecast and the action plan are very closely bound up together and the conclusions, therefore, may be conditional in that they outline several possible action plans, each with different implications in terms of profit, risk and capital required.

If the appraisal is taking place in order to enable an investment decision to be made, then the decision might well be one that is irreversible, or without an opportunity for reversal without appreciable financial loss. Sometimes it is possible to say about such an opportunity that it is likely to produce specified and worthwhile levels of profitability with little risk, or it is possible to form a definite adverse judgement. More commonly it is necessary to make a qualified conclusion stating, for example, that an investment is justified if certain particular actions are taken in relation to the business, or if certain specified preconditions are satisfied.

Examples

One rarely finds a black and white situation, but all the shades of grey are usually represented from which the report will seek to capture the main pattern. A few examples may perhaps serve to illustrate this.

Need for technological change

One company being appraised prior to acquisition had achieved very rapid growth in a specialized industrial process. The company had been built up by an entrepreneur who was still quite young. It had been very successful in terms of both growth rate and profitability and now a much larger industrial conglomerate was considering its acquisition as a means of diversification. On paper everything looked good about the company. The appraisal essentially supported this, but gave two important additional pieces of information:

1 The company had grown very rapidly and did not have a strong management infrastructure or really sound management control information. Success depended on thrust and energy, mainly from the founder, but the company had now grown too big for that kind of management style. There was therefore a need for more formal methods of organization and control.

   The change would have to be gradual, and it was essential that the original owner should be retained while the transition was taking place. It was necessary, therefore, to estimate how far he would accept and work successfully with such a change in management style.

2 New materials and new processes were being developed to satisfy the same market; these provided better customer satisfaction than the ones provided by the process with which the company had built its reputation and past profitability. The transition to the new processes had only just started a year or two earlier, but some competitors were already much stronger than the company under review. The indication was, therefore, that the company was strongest in a declining product area and weakest in the growing product area, and between the two areas there was a considerable technological step. This was not of short-term concern, provided that required development work was put in hand reasonably quickly.

The appraisal, therefore, confirmed that the acquisition was potentially a sound one, but revealed a need for a management development programme and the extension of the product range into a field of higher technology. It also highlighted the need to retain the existing chief executive.

Down-turn apparent

A second example was superficially similar, in that the company had grown steadily and was profitable and had been built by a single entrepreneur. The financial figures looked very satisfactory and the business appeared to be a desirable acquisition.

Beneath the surface, however, there were a number of problems. The chief executive, who was a major shareholder, was already in his seventies. He had run the company for many years as an absolute autocrat, with the result that all the other senior managers, several of whom were directors of the company, were unused to taking any but trivial decisions. The fact that they had accepted the situation for so long made it unlikely that they would suddenly change and become a powerful management force.

The company, which produced engineering capital goods, had in its earlier, more vigorous days, obtained a near monopoly in several important markets. There was, however, evidence that this situation was about to end. A visual examination of its products indicated that design methods were becoming outdated; for example, the mechanism was almost all in metal, much of it brass, and there was hardly any plastic used. A comparison with competitive products indicated that considerable cost reductions could have been achieved by using more modern materials and methods, without any loss of product durability or reliability. The products were, in a word, old-fashioned. The company was living on its past.

The appraisal revealed these problems and the subsequent report outlined them and recommended that an acquisition should take place only if the acquiring company had considerable spare management capacity and was prepared to rationalize the development engineering function and embark on an immediate programme of product renewal. After considering the report it was decided not to make the acquisition.

The business was acquired shortly afterwards by another engineering company and, for at least three years thereafter, their annual report referred to severe problems of this particular subsidiary company. This, therefore, was a case in which an appraisal reversed the impression of the financial figures and indicated that the company was at a downward turning point in its performance.

Successful vertical growth

Another example illustrates the reverse situation in which an apparently high risk investment proved to be a sound proposition. The company in this case was involved in the mail order sales of a limited range of products, which they purchased from a dozen or so manufacturers. The company had been discussing with a merchant bank the provision of additional capital in order to finance the establishment of its own manufacturing facility. The bank doubted that the company was capable of successfully entering manufacturing and it seemed unlikely that the funds would be forthcoming. However, it was decided that an appraisal was justified.

The appraisal showed that the business, whose growth rate had slowed down in the previous year or two, was being badly held back because of its dependence on subcontractors. In particular, the time taken to develop and introduce new products in response to market changes was too long and this was harming its competitive position. The plans to enter manufacture had been well prepared, and most important of all, an experienced executive had already been appointed by the company to head up the manufacturing operation.

The appraisal paid a great deal of attention to the rate at which the factory could reach a profitable production level using relatively raw labour and found that, although there would be a period of losses, even the pessimistic forecasts indicated satisfactory profitability within a year and, on a two or three year view, the investment was well justified. The company received its funds and subsequently substantially achieved its planned results.

Summary

Every business situation is unique and it is therefore dangerous to generalize, but it can be said that the most common features open to question during appraisal are:

1 The quality of the management resource.
2 The quality of the sales forecast.
3 The company's perception of its own distinctive competence.

The examples given indicate the main theme of this book, which is that whilst the company's past profit performance and its current balance sheet are essential indicators to future profit performance, they are far from sufficient. To come to worthwhile decisions about the profit potential of a company one must look beyond the balance sheet.

Chapter Sixteen

CONCLUSION

A thorough appraisal of profit potential of the kind discussed in this book can appreciably narrow the area of uncertainty in a wide category of business decisions. This benefit applies whether it is a matter of investing in a new project, acquiring a new business, developing an existing business, or even deciding to close a business and use the resources elsewhere. In all these circumstances and many others, a rounded study can provide the decision-maker with information based on objective analysis which will help him to make up his mind.

It will not, of course, replace the decision-making process; what it will do is to reduce the uncertainties in matters which can be factually resolved and suggest which of the indeterminant ones are crucial to the success of the project. It therefore allows a more informed decision to be made and one which is likely to be based on the real issues involved rather than those which appear superficially to be important.

It would be pleasant to be able to state that the predictions included in such appraisals will always be borne out by later events. The truth is, of course, that no-one can always be right however careful the appraisal. Changes in the economic environment are not all predictable; nor is government action, which is increasingly affecting the performance of individual sectors of industry. Highly competent individuals may make mistakes and their performance may decline for reasons that no appraisal could have foreseen. Competitors may make quite unexpected decisions, both favourable and unfavourable to the business under review. If a merger is under consideration it is never possible to predict with complete assurance the effect on an individual of working in a different management environment, even less the effect of one group of personalities on another. Some uncertainty will, therefore, always remain.

Of course, this is true of business as a whole. To be successful it is not necessary to be right all the time, but only to be right rather more often than wrong. Since success in business has far more to do with identifying and exploiting favourable opportunities than it has to do with solving problems, any company that is too cautious in its investment or acquisition programme is unlikely to expand at all, and may miss many attractive openings. Equally, one that is too adventurous will burden itself with unprofitable ventures that may easily nullify the beneficial effect of its successful investments.

There are, thus, two conflicting pressures: one which recognizes the need of a business to seize opportunities in order to expand; and the other which says 'if in doubt don't'. On the whole if it has been decided, as part of a company's objectives, that it will expand at a given rate, the more investment opportunities are considered, the more it will be possible to be selective. Other things being equal, it is always better to select the best five out of twenty opportunities, than the best five out of seven or eight.

The best approach therefore is to specify carefully what is expected from any investment, and appraise thoroughly all possibilities that seem to satisfy the requirements before a decision is made.

The evaluation of profit potential at frequent intervals is a necessary process for any growth business. To look beyond the balance sheet into the intrinsic qualities of the business in an attempt to discern its fundamental strengths and to estimate how effectively they will be utilized, is an essential part of such an evaluation.

BIBLIOGRAPHY

Ansoff, H. I., *Corporate strategy*, McGraw-Hill, London and New York (1965).

Bolt, G. J., *Market and sales forecasting*, Kogan Page, London (1972).

Drucker, P. F., *Managing for results*, Heinemann, London (1964).

Drucker, P. F., *The practice of management*, Heinemann, London (1955).

Levitt, T., *The marketing mode*, McGraw-Hill, London and New York (1969).

Linowes, D. F., *Managing growth through aquisition*, AMA, New York (1968).

Payne, B., *Planning for company growth*, McGraw-Hill, London and New York (1963).

Reynolds, W. H., *Products and markets*, Meredith, New York (1969).

Rockley, L. E., *Investment for profitability*, Business Books, London (1973).

Spitz, A. E., *Product planning*, Auerbach, London and New York (1972).

INDEX